## AMERICA *the* BEAUTIFUL

# NEBRASKA

By Jim Hargrove

### Consultants

**Dennis Lichty**, Social Studies Consultant, Nebraska Department of Education

**James E. Potter**, Historian, Nebraska State Historical Society; Editor, *Nebraska History*

**Robert L. Hillerich, Ph.D.,** Bowling Green State University, Bowling Green, Ohio

CHILDRENS PRESS ®

CHICAGO

**A dairy farm near Grand Island**

Project Editor: Joan Downing
Assistant Editor: Shari Joffe
Design Director: Margrit Fiddle
Typesetting: Graphic Connections, Inc.
Engraving: Liberty Photoengraving

Childrens Press®, Chicago

Library of Congress Cataloging-in-Publication Data

Hargrove, Jim.
    America the beautiful. Nebraska / by Jim Hargrove.
        p.    cm.
    Includes index.
    Summary: Introduces the geography, history,
government, economy, culture, famous sites, and people of
the Cornhusker State.
    ISBN 0-516-00473-5
    1.  Nebraska—Juvenile
literature.  [1.  Nebraska]  I.  Title.
F666.3.H37  1988                                        88-11746
978.2—dc19                                                    CIP
                                                                  AC

Winter on the plains

## TABLE OF CONTENTS

# Chapter 1

# AMERICA'S MAIN STREET

# AMERICA'S MAIN STREET

The name *Nebraska* comes from an Oto Indian word meaning "flat water." The Indians used the word to describe the Platte River, which flows across the state. It is fitting that the state is named after the Oto word for this river, because the river, its valley, and its tributaries have been central to the state's—and the nation's—growth and development.

For centuries, the Platte River provided water for the animals that lived on the plains. This, in turn, made the lands desirable hunting grounds for early Indians. Eventually, European explorers followed the river as they sought to learn about the land and its wealth. About 150 years ago, settlers surged westward across what is now Nebraska along the Platte and the North Platte rivers.

As pioneers traveled through the region, settlements grew along the river. These settlements provided goods and services for those who were just passing through, as well as for the local townspeople. The area soon became a "Main Street" for settlers and pioneers alike.

Irrigation and dry-farming methods have made Nebraska one of the nation's leading farming states. The Platte Valley has maintained its importance as a link in cross-country travel and as a distribution area for much of the nation's farm and ranch products. Interstate 80, the nation's most-traveled east-west highway, speeds through central Nebraska and the Platte Valley.

While many pioneers chose to travel through Nebraska, some decided to stay. For those who stayed, the state has revealed a charm unique among the states. And like many Main Streets, the state has provided a thoroughfare and a farmers' market for the surrounding population.

# Chapter 2
# THE LAND

# THE LAND

In her novel *My Antonia*, Willa Cather described her childhood home in rural Nebraska:

> We were talking about what it is like to spend one's childhood in little towns like these, buried in wheat and corn, under stimulating extremes of climate: burning summers when the world lies green and billowy beneath a brilliant sky, when one is fairly stifled in vegetation, in the colour and smell of strong weeds and heavy harvests; blustery winters with little snow, when the whole country is stripped bare and grey as sheet-iron. We agreed that no one who had not grown up in a little prairie town could know anything about it.

Willa Cather was born in Virginia and moved to Nebraska with her parents at the age of ten. At first, the flat, treeless grasslands of southern Nebraska made her homesick for the hills of Virginia. Her new home, she wrote, seemed "nothing but land: not a country at all, but the material out of which countries are made."

She soon changed her mind. She found in her adopted state a land of secret charms and surprising variety. Like many others, Willa Cather soon discovered that Nebraska was far more than just a way station on the great westward highway.

## GEOGRAPHY AND TOPOGRAPHY

Nebraska has a total area of 77,355 square miles (200,350 square kilometers), making it the fifteenth-largest state in the United States. At its widest distance from east to west, measured along a

Fertile grasslands cover the eastern third of Nebraska.

line extending from the Missouri River just south of Omaha to the state's western border, the state is about 415 miles (668 kilometers) across. Much of the northern and southern borders of the state are perfectly straight. The greatest north-south distance in Nebraska is 206 miles (331 kilometers). The state is located near the center of the continental United States.

Nebraska can be described as a series of great, rolling plateaus that rise from a low point of 840 feet (256 meters) above sea level in the southeast, to 5,426 feet (1,654 meters) above sea level in westernmost Kimball County. The slope of the land is generally constant: about 10 feet per mile (3 meters per kilometer).

The rich farmland of the eastern third of Nebraska is part of the nation's Central Lowlands region. This is the part of the state that receives the most rainfall, and the land, generally flat or gradually undulating, is ideal for farming. With advances in farming and intensive irrigation, the eastern farms have been able to support a

The rugged Badlands lie in Nebraska's northwestern corner.

large variety of crops. To the west and northwest is an enchanting region known as the Sand Hills, an area of 25- to 100-foot- (8- to 30-meter-) high sand hills covered by a variety of thick grasses. This region, dotted with small lakes, is well suited for grazing cattle.

Except for a relatively small area in the northwestern corner of the state known as the Badlands, most of western Nebraska is classified as High Plains. These plains, which stand about 3,000 to 4,000 feet (914 to 1,219 meters) above sea level, are occasionally broken by deep canyons.

## THE LAND IN ANCIENT TIMES

The various regions of Nebraska were formed at different times during the past 75 million years. Once, and perhaps several times, Nebraska's land was at the bottom of a great inland sea. Between

**Far-western Nebraska boasts such striking natural formations as Eagle Rock.**

75 million and 100 million years ago, great upheavals of the earth's surface resulted in the creation of the Rocky Mountains. Although the Rockies do not extend eastward into Nebraska, these movements of the earth's crust caused the land of Nebraska to slope down toward the east.

The northwest corner of the state, known as the Badlands, today looks much as it did 40 million years ago. This area is actually a continuation of the Badlands of neighboring South Dakota. This dry, desertlike land is punctuated by deep, twisted canyons, sandstone buttes, rocky mounds shaped like cones, and oddly balanced rocks. It is hard to imagine that, millions of years ago, this area was formed by torrents of water rushing away from higher land.

The Sand Hills lie north of the Platte River in the central part of the state.

The Sand Hills of north-central Nebraska have a different, far more recent origin. Between two thousand and five thousand years ago, the Sand Hills were formed by winds picking up sand from the beds of dried rivers. Scientists believe that for several thousand years, this area looked somewhat like portions of the Sahara Desert, with large dunes pushed into ever-changing shapes by the force of the wind. The Sand Hills of Nebraska make up the largest system of dunes in the Western Hemisphere, covering about 20,000 square miles (51,800 square kilometers). Although the area is dry, it looks little like a desert today. Some scientists believe that the grasses that now cover the dunes began growing as recently as five hundred years ago.

Some of the fertile farmland of eastern Nebraska was shaped hundreds of thousands of years ago, when Ice Age glaciers moved through the eastern fifth of the state and left behind fertile soil traced by several rivers.

Toadstool Park (left) has yielded a large number of animal fossils, many of which are on display at Morrill Hall in Lincoln (above).

## A FOSSIL HUNTER'S DREAMLAND

Sioux County, in the extreme northwest corner of the state, is one of the richest sources of fossils in the United States. The fossilized remains of ancient animals found here indicate that Nebraska, at least during some eras, was a tropical land. Around Toadstool Park, in the northern portion of the county, fossils of saber-toothed tigers, rhinoceroses, camels, turtles, crocodiles, and many other animals have been found. Many of these animals thrived only in a tropical climate.

To the south of Toadstool Park, still within the deserted wilds of Sioux County, is another important area of concentrated fossil remains. Agate Fossil Beds National Monument is the second-richest source of fossils in the United States. At this important historical site, visitors can see fossil remains of strange prehistoric animals that roamed the area as early as 20 million years ago, such as mastodons and huge pigs. The area also contains evidence

15

of more recent life forms, including fossils of bison from nearly ten thousand years ago.

Nebraska is well known as a rich source of fossils. The world's largest mammoth fossil was found in the state, and the University of Nebraska boasts one of the largest paleontological (fossil) museums in the United States.

## RIVERS, LAKES, AND UNDERGROUND WATER

To much of America, Nebraska's most famous river is the Missouri, which forms the entire eastern border of the state and a small portion of the northern border. The "Mighty Mo," as the river is sometimes called, meanders along the Nebraska border for about 450 miles (724 kilometers). Every stream and river in the state eventually empties into the wide Missouri.

To generations of Nebraskans and pioneers who traveled through the state, the Platte River symbolized the history of Nebraska. The Platte was America's highway westward, its branches leading all the way to the Rocky Mountains.

The Platte River varies from half a mile (.8 kilometers) to nearly a full mile (1.6 kilometers) in width, but in recent times, dams and irrigation systems have reduced its flow. It is a very shallow river. In the spring, its depth may vary from 1 to 6 feet (.3 to 1.8 meters); in summer, portions of it may dry up entirely. Early settlers liked to call the Platte the "mile-wide, inch-deep river."

Two separate rivers join to form the Platte: the North Platte, which flows southeastward from Wyoming; and the South Platte, which flows northeastward from Colorado. The two rivers join to form the Platte at the town of North Platte in west-central Nebraska. The Platte flows eastward through the state until it reaches the Missouri River. More than half of Nebraska's total land area is drained by the Platte and its major tributaries, which include the Loup and Elkhorn rivers.

Other major rivers in the state are the Republican River, near the southern border; the Big Blue, Little Blue, Big Nemaha, and Little Nemaha, in the southeast; and the Elkhorn and the Niobrara, in the north. The Niobrara is a swift-running river that flows through some of the state's most scenic regions. All of these rivers eventually empty into the Missouri.

Most of Nebraska's nearly two thousand lakes are in the northern portion of the state. The majority lie in the Sand Hills region. The state has few large natural lakes. The biggest lakes in Nebraska have been formed by dams along a number of the state's rivers. The largest is Lake McConaughy, which covers about 55 square miles (142 square kilometers) and is formed by a dam on the North Platte River.

The small lakes and rivers that dot the Sand Hills region are not the area's only water source. About 2,000 square miles (5,180 square kilometers) of the area are situated above the enormous Ogallala Aquifer, one of the largest reservoirs of underground water in the United States. This supply of groundwater in the Sand Hills keeps the Loup and Elkhorn rivers flowing all year round. The Ogallala Aquifer and similar but smaller reserves of underground water throughout the region provide irrigation and well water for many of the state's farmers. However, depletion and even contamination of the underground water system has raised concerns about the future of such water supplies.

## CLIMATE

Along with its neighboring states, Nebraska has what is called a "continental" or "interior" climate—a polite way of saying that

Violent storms and extreme shifts in temperature can occur suddenly in Nebraska.

the winters are often bitter cold and the summers burning hot. Air from the Gulf of Mexico or the Pacific Ocean must travel at least 1,000 miles (1,609 kilometers) to reach Nebraska. As it travels overland, the air is easily warmed in the summer and cooled in the winter.

Summertime can bring intense and prolonged heat. During an average summer, portions of southern Nebraska can expect at least forty to fifty days of temperatures above 90 degrees Fahrenheit (32 degrees Celsius). Summer temperatures in excess of 100 degrees Fahrenheit (38 degrees Celsius) are common.

The highest temperature ever recorded in Nebraska was a blistering 118 degrees Fahrenheit (48 degrees Celsius). Three towns share the record: Geneva, on July 15, 1934; Hartington, on July 17, 1936; and Minden, on July 24, 1936. At the other extreme, the lowest recorded temperature was minus 47 degrees Fahrenheit (minus 44 degrees Celsius), near Northport, on February 12, 1899.

Nebraska is sometimes beset by other weather extremes. When warm air from the Gulf of Mexico collides with cool air from the north, the results can be very unpredictable. Tornadoes, blizzards, violent electrical storms, and hail are some of the weather extremes experienced by Nebraskans.

The western portions of Nebraska frequently receive less than eighteen inches (forty-six centimeters) of rainfall each year. Portions of eastern Nebraska average more than twenty-seven inches (sixty-nine centimeters) each year. The eastern part of the state averages about thirty inches (seventy-six centimeters) of snowfall yearly; the west receives somewhat less. The relative humidity averages 60 percent from April to October and 70 percent from November to March.

## WORKING WITH THE LAND

Extremes of temperature and scant precipitation have created a hardy and resourceful brand of Nebraskan farmer. In the west, where the light rainfall is not sufficient for growing corn, farmers grow such crops as wheat and sugar beets, which can be sustained with less water. Thousands of cattle graze and fatten on the hardy grasses of the Sand Hills region.

In the east, where rainfall is more plentiful, farmers grow corn, soybeans, and other crops; and raise livestock such as hogs and poultry. Irrigation is carried out throughout much of the state, making a land that was once mistakenly called the "Great American Desert" a rich farmland and a leader in farm income.

"We come and go, but the land is always here," wrote Willa Cather, "and the people who love it and understand it are the people who own it—for a little while."

# Chapter 3
# THE PEOPLE

# THE PEOPLE

"Nebraska farmers have a little different attitude toward life than many other persons," wrote Mrs. Ardis Bleyhl in *Nebraska Farmer* magazine. "Perhaps it is because, in a highly mobile society, we [Nebraskans] tend to 'stay put,' with close ties to our homes, our families, and our communities."

A perfect example of her theory, Mrs. Bleyhl was living in a farmhouse that was built by her grandfather in 1879. Both she and her father were born in the house. But not every Nebraskan lives on a farm or ranch. In recent years, an increasing percentage of the state's residents have chosen to live in cities and towns.

## POPULATION

Nebraska is a relatively large state with a fairly small population. According to the 1980 census, it had 1,569,825 residents, making it thirty-fifth among the states in population. Between 1970 and 1980, the state's total population grew by just under 6 percent, whereas the population of the nation as a whole grew 11.45 percent. Population estimates in 1985 indicated that Nebraska may soon slip to the rank of thirty-sixth most-populous state.

Although the state swelled with immigrants during the nineteenth century, about 98 percent of today's residents were born in the United States. The state has a relatively small number of members of minority groups. According to a 1985 estimate, the

A Swedish Festival is held every June in Stromsburg.

state had 1,490,381 whites, 48,390 blacks, 28,025 Hispanics, 9,145 American Indians, and 21,909 people classified as "other." However, many of the recent ancestors of today's Nebraskans were foreign born. In the nineteenth century, thousands of German, Scandinavian, Czech, and Irish immigrants flocked to the state in search of free or inexpensive land. Many came in response to advertisements placed in Europe by the builders of the transcontinental railroad. Omaha is the center of black culture in Nebraska, and most of Nebraska's blacks live either in Omaha or Lincoln.

Sixty-six percent of Nebraskans live in urban areas. The largest urban areas are located in the eastern part of the state. The population is especially dense around the state's two largest cities, Omaha and Lincoln. Forty-four percent of all Nebraskans live in one of these two metropolitan areas, which are less than sixty miles (ninety-seven kilometers) apart. The few densely populated areas in the west are located along the Platte and North Platte rivers.

Away from the Platte River in north and central Nebraska are some counties that average less than five residents per square mile (less than two residents per square kilometer). In these strangely beautiful areas, it seems almost as if humanity has vanished, leaving behind dirt or gravel roads, an occasional barbed-wire fence, and perhaps an old windmill in the distance.

The population of Nebraska is overwhelmingly Christian. Protestant groups include Lutherans, Methodists, and Presbyterians. Roman Catholics make up the largest single religious group in the state. Many of the state's first immigrants came in groups sponsored by religious organizations.

## TOWN AND COUNTRY

Many of the people who live in Nebraska's cities and large towns work in industries as diverse as food packaging, insurance, and transportation. Omaha is an important center for the insurance and transportation industries. Many insurance companies are headquartered in Lincoln as well.

Nebraska is centrally located in the continental United States, and Omaha was the eastern terminus of the first transcontinental railroad. These two factors helped to nurture a flourishing transportation industry in Omaha. The Union Pacific Railroad, one of two companies that built the transcontinental railroad, is still headquartered in Omaha.

Nebraskans who live in and around such cities and towns as Grand Island, Fremont, Kearney, Hastings, Scottsbluff, and McCook are much like residents of other large urban and suburban areas. They work in offices, retail stores, or in large

A participant in the cattle-judging contest at the Grant County Fair near Hyannis in the Sand Hills

industries, and their children attend modern schools. These urban dwellers drive on efficient highways and may choose from a wide variety of cultural diversions, including theaters, movies, museums, and fine restaurants.

Away from Nebraska's cities and towns, however, life may be very different. Genuine cowboys can still be found in Nebraska, although they are more often called ranchers and ranch hands. On some huge cattle ranches in northern and western Nebraska, horses are still a necessity. "We still do much of our cattle work with horses," a Nebraska rancher told *National Geographic* magazine a few years ago. "Out there in the summer range you can tear up expensive equipment pretty fast. Besides, horses are self-supporting, and on this large a ranch you're a long way ahead using them for much of the work with cattle."

The Sand Hills region, in particular, is home to the modern cowboy. Country-and-western is the type of music one is most likely to hear on the radio stations there. On summer weekends, ranch hands and ranchers often can be seen driving pickup trucks to local rodeos. On desolate roads in Nebraska's back country, away from the Platte Valley, it is not uncommon to see students

Nebraska's Native Americans have made rich contributions to the state's culture.

riding in pickup trucks and cars for their daily commute to and from school. Some students have to travel as far as fifty miles (eighty kilometers) to get to school.

In some rural parts of the state, a few people still live in sod houses—structures made of grass and earth that are much like those built more than a century ago by Nebraska pioneers. However, nineteenth-century pioneers would scarcely recognize these now-rare sod houses, for most of them are covered with siding or stucco and boast such modern conveniences as electricity and indoor plumbing.

## NATIVE AMERICANS

Nebraska's Native American, or American Indian, population is scattered throughout the state. The Omaha Reservation centers around Macy; the Winnebago Reservation lies just to the north. Descendants of the Santee Sioux live in the region around Santee and Niobrara. The Pine Ridge country of northwestern Nebraska also has a small Indian population. In addition, both Omaha and Lincoln have active, growing American Indian centers that provide cultural experiences, educational opportunities, and job counseling.

Chapter 4

# THE FIRST NEBRASKANS

# THE FIRST NEBRASKANS

Archaeological evidence indicates that as early as twelve thousand years ago, nomadic groups of Native Americans, referred to by scholars as Paleo-Indians, roamed the land that is now Nebraska. Archaeologists named one such group the Folsom Culture because the stone knives and spear or arrow tips of these people were first discovered near Folsom, New Mexico. People of the Folsom and other early cultures are believed to have lived in the western part of Nebraska, as well as in other neighboring states.

Paleo-Indians hunted large game, but the animals they encountered so long ago on the Great Plains were vastly different from those living there today. Ancient, fossilized animal bones found near Folsom Culture artifacts indicate that giant sloths, long-extinct species of bison, varieties of camel, and a native North American species of horse once roamed the plains and were hunted by early Paleo-Indians. For unknown reasons, the horse disappeared entirely from the New World, and did not reappear until the domestic European horse was introduced by Spanish explorers.

## ANCIENT INDIANS OF NEBRASKA

The oldest Indian remains in Nebraska are from the Folsom Culture. Archaeological finds indicate that other Indians, who were part of what is called the Archaic Culture, lived in the area from about 5000 B.C. to A.D. 1. Excavations near Signal Butte in western Nebraska have uncovered one such culture that, like the Folsom Culture, was made up of hunters who had little or no agriculture. However, the people of the Archaic Culture hunted a wider variety of animals than did the Paleo-Indians, and supplemented their hunting by gathering wild plants.

Evidence of the first known earthen pottery made by Nebraska Indians dates from approximately 100 B.C. to A.D. 900, a time archaeologists call the Woodland Period. These people made simple pottery, were probably less nomadic than earlier cultures, and probably grew a few crops such as squash and gourds. The simple pottery found in Nebraska is similar to pottery found in the eastern United States, indicating that these Indians may have migrated to Nebraska from the woodlands and forests of the East. For this reason, they are referred to as Woodland Indians.

Over a long period of time, but still before the first Europeans reached the New World, other groups of Indians migrated to Nebraska and other parts of the Great Plains region. These newcomers brought a more-developed civilization to the area. For many of the groups, farming joined hunting as a means of obtaining food. For the first time, maize (a type of corn) and beans were grown and harvested. Some of these groups built large, permanent, earthen lodges. The floors of these large homes were often built below the surface of the ground.

One of these groups is referred to as the Upper Republican Culture. These people lived along the banks of the Republican River in southern Nebraska, as well as along the Loup River in the central part of the state. A similar group was the Nebraska Culture, which inhabited villages along the Missouri River. The Indians of these cultures lived in villages of perhaps fifty to one

Corn was a staple food for the Indians of the Great Plains.

hundred people. They developed fairly sophisticated agricultural techniques. Planting sticks were used to dig holes in the ground for planting corn, and bones from the shoulders of bison were used as hoes. Underground storage pits were built to store surplus grain. Although these Indians grew much of their food, they still occasionally left their villages to hunt the bison that roamed the Great Plains.

## THE CHANGING PLAINS

Virtually all the information about the native people of North America who lived before the arrival of Europeans comes from the interpretation of archaeological evidence. Many of the first Europeans to arrive in the New World were eager to observe the American Indians they encountered. Several explorers and settlers wrote about the Indians, providing us with some of the earliest firsthand descriptions of the Indian way of life. But the arrival of

**Horses, introduced to North America by the Spanish, enabled the Plains Indians to hunt migrating herds of buffalo.**

the Europeans did more than improve our contemporary understanding of early Native Americans. It also began a long period of nearly constant change for the Indians of North America—including the Indians of the Great Plains.

Early in the seventeenth century, probably before 1630, the Spanish reintroduced horses to North America. By the middle of the next century, horses could be found in abundance throughout the Great Plains. The horse revolutionized life for the Indians of Nebraska. For the first time, the great herds of buffalo could be followed and hunted. Horses allowed Indians on the Nebraska plains to travel more extensively than ever before. The desirability of the horse also encouraged a sophisticated system of trade among the Indians. But the arrival of European settlers in America created problems for Nebraska Indians even before the settlers reached the Great Plains. As civilizations transplanted from Europe began developing in the East, eastern Indians were forced onto new lands in the West. Competition for valuable resources

In the 1600s, as Indian groups in the East were forced westward by the advancing European settlers, and as the Indians began to acquire European horses and firearms, warfare between the Indians of the Great Plains intensified.

began to arise in such areas as Nebraska. Around the same time, horses were brought to the plains, and firearms were introduced by Indians who obtained them from Spanish and French explorers. Guns and horses revolutionized Indian warfare, which became more intense because of the approaching white settlers.

## NEBRASKA INDIANS IN THE EIGHTEENTH CENTURY

When white explorers first entered Nebraska in the early 1700s, several groups of Indians lived or hunted within the state's current borders. Among these groups were the Arapahoes, Cheyennes, Missouris, Omahas, Otos, Pawnees, Oncas, and Sioux. The Pawnees, who settled along the Platte, Republican, and Loup rivers, were the largest group. Although the white explorers probably did not realize it, many of the Indian tribes they

Nineteenth-century artist George Catlin, who spent much of his career observing Plains Indians, recorded this impression of a group of Pawnees.

encountered were relative newcomers to the area that is now Nebraska.

Ancestors of the Pawnees had come to central Nebraska and Kansas from the south and the east. They built large, earth-covered lodges along riverbanks, and grew corn, squash, and beans. Like other eastern Nebraska Indians, especially the Oto and Omaha tribes, the Pawnees frequently left their villages to hunt buffalo. When they traveled great distances, they carried cone-shaped, animal-skin tepees with them. The Pawnee and Omaha Indians also developed some of the most sophisticated poetry, songs, and religious ceremonies of all the Indians of the Great Plains.

The Pawnees were regarded as fierce fighters by some of their Indian neighbors. The Sioux who lived to the north, however, considered themselves superior to the Pawnees. In general, the Pawnees did not pose a great threat to the white settlers who began entering Nebraska in the 1800s. During the 1860s and

While in their villages, the Omahas lived in log-framed, sod-covered earth lodges.

1870s, some Pawnees enlisted as scouts in the United States Army's battles against the Sioux.

The western Sioux Indians were part of an enormous confederation of tribes that once inhabited most of the area between the Great Lakes and the Dakotas. The Sioux sometimes used the plains of western Nebraska as hunting grounds.

The Sioux, the Arapahoes, and the Cheyennes were nomadic hunters who roamed the plains of western Nebraska hunting buffalo. They built no permanent villages and gathered vegetation rather than growing crops. They depended heavily on the buffalo for food, as well as for much of their clothing. Although these hunters made no pottery, their animal skins and personal objects were frequently decorated with lovely, elaborate geometric designs.

The Ponca, Oto, Omaha, and Missouri Indians lived along riverbanks, mostly in eastern Nebraska. The Omaha Indians, whose name was eventually adopted by Nebraska's largest city, were representative of these cultures. Living in permanent villages roughly between the Platte, Niobrara, and Missouri rivers, the Omaha built large earth- and bark-covered lodges, and cultivated corn and other vegetables. Like the Pawnees, the Omaha Indians carried cone-shaped tepees with them when they left their villages to hunt buffalo.

Virtually all of the feared hunter-warrior Indians of Nebraska led relatively peaceful lives before Europeans began to settle in the New World. Until the start of the eighteenth century, the Arapahoes and Cheyennes lived in the Minnesota and North Dakota regions. In the early 1700s, these people were forced from their homelands by the Sioux. The Sioux had been forced from their permanent villages in the Great Lakes region by the Chippewa Indians, who had obtained European guns from the French.

Most of the Indian peoples who were considered by the Europeans to be nomadic hunters and warriors were, in reality, refugees living in western Nebraska. Many were originally farmers who had been evicted from their previous lands and forced to roam the plains of Nebraska. Their wandering existence, based almost exclusively on buffalo hunting, was a recent development. Even the Pawnee and Oto Indians, who managed to keep their villages until they were finally driven out by white settlers during the nineteenth century, were forced to adopt new life-styles with the coming of the Europeans.

One of the most unfortunate consequences of the arrival of European settlers was that they brought with them diseases, such as smallpox, that had never before existed in North America. In the early 1800s, huge numbers of Pawnee and Omaha Indians were wiped out by diseases to which they had no immunities.

# Chapter 5
# THE EXPLORERS

# THE EXPLORERS

No one is certain who was the first white man to set foot on the land of present-day Nebraska. In 1540, Spanish explorer Francisco Vásquez de Coronado led an expedition of about three hundred Spanish soldiers and many Indians northeastward from Mexico into the central portion of the Great Plains. By 1541, Coronado's band had traveled as far north as Kansas, just south of present-day Nebraska. Unable to locate the fabulous city of gold that was rumored to exist in the Great Plains region, Coronado went no farther. After claiming vast amounts of territory for Spain, including the land of present-day Nebraska, he returned to Mexico.

Coronado's expedition gave Spain a shadowy claim to the Great Plains. However, this claim was not recognized by the other colonial powers fighting for control of North America. By the early 1600s, the English colonies along the Atlantic coast claimed the same land—even though no English colonist had ever seen it. By the mid-1600s, French colonists and fur traders were establishing colonies in Canada. They soon began to move west and south in search of valuable beaver pelts, which had become popular as a material for clothing and hats.

French explorer René-Robert Cavelier, Sieur de La Salle, traveled down the Mississippi River in 1681. In 1682, he claimed for France all the lands drained by the Mississippi River and its tributaries—an area that covered about the central third of the present-day United States and included Nebraska. He named this vast territory Louisiana in honor of French king Louis XIV.

So, by the close of the seventeenth century, present-day Nebraska was claimed for Spain by Coronado, who probably never quite reached it; for France by La Salle, who certainly never reached it; and for England by various English colonialists, who never even set out to reach it.

## COLONIAL SOLDIERS

In 1712, Étienne Veniard de Bourgmont, the commander of the French fort at Detroit, deserted his post in order to live with Missouri Indians living west of the Mississippi River. Two years later, he traveled by boat up the Missouri River to the Platte River.

Bourgmont's presence, as well as reports of French trappers in the territory claimed by Spain, concerned the Spanish colonial militia at Santa Fe, New Mexico. In the summer of 1719, Governor Valverde of New Mexico set out for the South Platte River in search of Frenchmen trespassing on what he considered to be Spanish land. Although Valverde encountered no French settlers, a group of Indians told him that they had seen villages on the South Platte that had been built by whites. Winter was approaching, and Valverde hurried back to Santa Fe.

In the summer of the following year, a group of forty-two Spanish soldiers and about sixty Indians set out from Santa Fe under the command of Captain Pedro de Villasur. The Spanish troops were determined to drive French settlers out of the Platte Valley. On August 13, 1720, Villasur's troops camped where the Loup River enters the Platte, near present-day Columbus, Nebraska.

This painting, a facsimile of an eighteenth-century work done on buffalo hide, shows the confrontation that occurred in the Platte Valley in 1720 between Pawnee Indians and Spanish troops led by Pedro de Villasur.

Early that evening, the Spanish soldiers were attacked by Pawnee Indians who were possibly being aided by the French. Only about a dozen of Villasur's soldiers escaped death in the brief battle. The Indians took most of the Spaniards' belongings, including their fine horses, which were then added to the Pawnees' growing herd. For the next century and a half, the Pawnees owned the finest horses of any Plains Indians.

Despite Spanish claims to the region, Frenchmen continued to explore the area that is now Nebraska. Most notable were two brothers, Pierre and Paul Mallet, who crossed the region in 1739 and 1740.

Over the next two decades, the French and the Spanish continued to argue over who owned the vast territory that the French called Louisiana and that included what is now Nebraska.

In 1763, by the terms of the treaty that ended the French and Indian War, Spain was officially given all of Louisiana west of the Mississippi River. France gave up its claim to the entire Louisiana territory—but not for long.

In 1800, Emperor Napoleon of France secretly persuaded Spain to cede Louisiana back to France. Three years later, the United States government, under the leadership of President Thomas Jefferson, purchased Louisiana from France for only $15 million. The Louisiana Purchase of 1803 was probably the best real-estate deal in history. The land of present-day Nebraska now belonged to the United States.

## THE LEWIS AND CLARK EXPEDITION

In July 1804, a group of about forty-five men under the command of Meriwether Lewis and William Clark reached the mouth of the Platte River. The expedition had been sent by President Jefferson to explore the Louisiana Territory by following the Missouri River. When they reached the Platte River, Lewis and Clark sent two men on horseback to find the villages of the Oto and Pawnee Indians who were thought to live along the river. When the two men returned, they reported that most of the Indians were away on a buffalo hunt. A third messenger, a man named Barter who claimed to speak a little of the Oto language, was sent to find the traveling Indians. Although Barter never returned, Oto and Pawnee Indians eventually visited Lewis and Clark's camp.

Early in August of 1804, Lewis and Clark held a meeting with a group of Oto and Pawnee Indians at a spot along the Missouri River near present-day Omaha. The explorers told the Indians that there was a new "Great Father" in Washington, D.C. Hoping

Following the Missouri River, Meriwether Lewis (left) and William Clark (above) explored the eastern edge of Nebraska in 1804.

to establish a means by which whites could communicate with and ultimately govern the local Indians, Lewis and Clark recognized six Indian men as tribal leaders. However, the men chosen by Lewis and Clark did not have leadership status among their own people. For the first time, the Indians were being asked to submit to the rule of chiefs whom they had not themselves selected.

The newly appointed leaders were warned that if they did not govern properly, other leaders would be chosen by the whites who represented the government in Washington, D.C. In his report, Clark named the place of this early meeting "Council Bluff." Today, Fort Atkinson stands at the approximate location of Council Bluff.

In August of 1804, Lewis and Clark met with a group of Indians at a spot along the Missouri River that Clark later called Council Bluff.

The Lewis and Clark Expedition continued up the Missouri, which was noticeably more shallow now that they were above the point at which water flowed in from the Platte. Clark noted that there were large catfish in the river, and that deer, elk, and small game watched from the shores as the boats passed.

On the short journey up the Missouri to the villages of the Omaha Indians, the expedition passed the grave of Omaha Indian chief Black Bird. Black Bird and some of his followers, it was claimed, had been river pirates, taking valuables from every trader who traveled on the river. Lewis and Clark climbed the hill where Black Bird was buried and planted an American flag at the top.

The expedition soon reached an old Omaha village of about three hundred earthen lodges. The village had been burned and was virtually deserted. Four years earlier, smallpox had destroyed

Stephen Long (above) and John C. Frémont (right) were among those sent to explore Nebraska during the first half of the nineteenth century.

nearly half of the entire population of the tribe. Some Omaha Indians, as well as several Otos, eventually came to meet the white explorers. Lewis and Clark appointed more leaders for the local Indian tribes. In August, the expedition left the area that is now Nebraska.

## THE FIRST WAVE OF AMERICANS

Many American soldiers, explorers, and fur traders followed Lewis and Clark's expedition into the Nebraska wilderness. In 1806, Lieutenant Zebulon Pike traveled through parts of southern Nebraska, holding several meetings with Indians. Later explorers, all of them members of the United States military, included Major Stephen Long, who traveled through Nebraska in 1819 and 1820; Colonel Henry Dodge, who visited in 1835; and Lieutenant John C. Frémont, who explored the area from 1842 to 1844.

The Bordeaux Trading Post near Chadron, established in the early 1800s, now houses the Museum of the Fur Trade.

American soldiers were sent to Nebraska primarily to limit the influence the British might have over the Indians. American fur traders were anxious to establish business with the Indians without interference from the British. The Americans were interested in trading for buffalo skins, which could be made into valuable robes. They also prized the pelts of beavers and other fur-bearing animals that were plentiful between the Missouri River and the Rocky Mountains.

Around 1809, traders Ramsay Crooks and Robert McClellan built a fur-trading post on the west bank of the Missouri River north of the present site of Omaha. Over the next few years, a Spanish American trader named Manuel Lisa built several more posts along the river. In 1823, Andrew Drips of the Missouri Fur Company began operating a trading post near Bellevue. Posts also sprang up at Bellevue in 1827, and near Chadron, in the northwest corner of present-day Nebraska, in 1837.

**Fur traders and their guides approaching an Indian camp**

## FORT ATKINSON

When the men of the Lewis and Clark expedition met with the Indians at Council Bluff, they recommended construction of a United States military fort at the site. Many American politicians, including President James Monroe and Secretary of War John Calhoun, were anxious to demonstrate to Indians and British traders how much control the United States government had over the area along the upper Missouri River. Congress set aside money to establish a chain of American forts along the Missouri as far north and west as the mouth of the Yellowstone River, near the present-day border between Montana and North Dakota.

Calhoun ordered General Henry Atkinson to form an expedition to travel up the Missouri and build a fort at the mouth of the Yellowstone. In the winter of 1818-19, General Atkinson assembled more than a thousand troops and a fleet of four steamboats in the hope of carrying out what would become known as the Yellowstone Expedition.

In her book *The Beaver Men,* Nebraska author Mari Sandoz described the early days of the adventure:

> General Atkinson finally got his force of over a thousand men and their supplies on four steamboats. . . . The engines blew pistons, the boats sprang leaks, and caught on snags and sawyers. Two never got into the Missouri River at all, and only one made it to the mouth of the Kansas River, and stopped, the first alarm of the Indians turning to whoops and laughter when the fiery monster pounded and roared like a great crippled bug dying in the water.

None of the original four boats of the Yellowstone Expedition was able to reach even Council Bluff. A fifth, the *Western Engineer,* which was designed especially for travel on rivers like the Missouri and was sent to rescue the expedition, reached Council Bluff in September 1819. The *Western Engineer* was also carrying the exploration party of Major Stephen Long. The troops under General Atkinson's command finally arrived at Council Bluff in keelboats dragged by towlines from the shore.

With winter approaching, Atkinson postponed plans to continue up the Missouri. In 1819, his men began building a fort at the place Lewis and Clark had recommended. Eventually, this fort was named after him.

Fort Atkinson was the earliest frontier military post built west of the Missouri River. For its day, the fort was huge; the exterior dimensions of the outer wall were 455 feet by 468 feet (139 meters

Fort Atkinson, the earliest American frontier military post west
of the Missouri River, has been reconstructed.

by 143 meters). During its relatively short but active history, more
than a thousand soldiers were stationed there at any given time.

The fort allowed United States Army troops to keep a watchful
eye on the flourishing trade that was developing between
American traders and the Indians of the area. The fort also became
the site of Nebraska's first school, farm, library, sawmill, and
hospital.

However, despite its size and economic and social importance,
Fort Atkinson was abandoned in 1827, just eight years after it was
built. The troops stationed there were moved south to protect
trade along the developing Santa Fe Trail. In the meantime,
Congress had reversed its decision to fund the string of forts.
Withdrawal of support left Fort Atkinson as the only evidence of
the ambitious plan.

# Chapter 6

# ON THE ROAD TO STATEHOOD

# ON THE ROAD TO STATEHOOD

During the early decades of the 1800s, most of the people living permanently on the land that would become Nebraska were Indians. Many more people, primarily whites, lived there only temporarily or merely traveled through the area. This transient population included traders, soldiers, explorers, and missionaries.

## WAGONS ALONG THE PLATTE

In 1813, Robert Stuart led a party of Americans through the Platte Valley on his return from Oregon. Stuart and the people with him were the first Americans to travel the natural route that the North Platte and the Platte rivers afforded through the Great Plains. This path was part of what soon became known as the Oregon Trail.

A dozen years later, William Ashley led a group of fur trappers and traders along this route on their way to the Rocky Mountains. Other trappers and traders soon followed the same route west. In 1835, the first group of Christian missionaries bound for Oregon traveled along the Oregon Trail.

Missionaries and trappers who traveled west through the Platte Valley were the vanguard of a nation on the move. In 1843, a wagon train of more than a thousand settlers bound for Oregon rumbled through the Platte Valley along the Oregon Trail, signaling the start of an enormous westward movement that

In the 1840s and 1850s, about five hundred thousand pioneers migrated westward through Nebraska along the Oregon Trail, shown here as it appears today near Scottsbluff.

became known as the "Great Migration." Over the next fifteen years, an estimated five hundred thousand pioneers crossed Nebraska in covered wagons.

One of the most famous of these migrations occurred in 1847, when Brigham Young led about 150 Mormons on another route along the Platte on the way to the Great Salt Lake Valley. Over the next year, several thousand more Mormon pioneers followed Young's route, which became known as the Mormon Trail.

Few pioneers traveling through Nebraska considered staying there. The United States government had declared Nebraska to be Indian land, and whites were prohibited from settling there. Besides, most pioneers, lured by stories of lush lands and other riches, wished to go farther west. The government did try to assist

Following a route that became known as the Mormon Trail, Mormon pioneers traveled through Nebraska on their way to the Great Salt Lake Valley.

and protect the pioneers traveling through the valley. In 1846, the federal government established Fort Kearny at Table Creek near the present site of Nebraska City. It was soon clear, however, that this fort was too far from the westward routes to be effective. A second Fort Kearny was built along the Platte River in 1848, and the original fort was abandoned.

At Fort Kearny, a number of trails from the East came together to form the "Great Platte River Road." The route became a part of the Oregon Trail, the Mormon Trail, and the California Trail. For the majority of pioneers, Fort Kearny was the first important landmark west of the Missouri River.

An Oglala Sioux chief and his braves smoke a peace pipe as a wagon train on its way to California fords the south fork of the Platte River.

## THE MISUNDERSTOOD INDIANS OF THE PLAINS

Some movies and television shows about America's frontier days have given millions of people false impressions of the Plains Indians. A common scene shows white settlers traveling westward in wagon trains along such routes as the Oregon Trail. Suddenly, the pioneers are attacked by Indian warriors riding swift horses and wielding bows and arrows.

In reality, such scenes were rare. Wagon trains were usually heavily armed, and Indians rarely risked attacking them. At the time, the Indians probably did not realize that these early settlers were only the beginning of a human wave that would soon engulf their traditional hunting grounds. In later years, Indians would attack isolated Nebraska settlements and homesteads, but those hostilities lasted only a few decades. The often-told tales of mounted Indian warriors battling for their lands and hunting grounds describes only a very brief period in the history of a people that spans twelve thousand years.

# DIARY OF AN OREGON TRAIL PIONEER

A number of the pioneers who traveled through the Platte Valley in the mid-1800s kept personal diaries in which they recorded their impressions of the long journey. One such pioneer was Enoch W. Conyers, who passed through the Platte Valley in 1852 on his way to Oregon. A few excerpts from his diary are reprinted here:

April 20, 1852—It was an ideal spring morning, the sun shining its very brightest . . . when about ten o'clock our long journey across the plains was commenced. Our wagon, secured especially for the trip, was light and of the very best material; our team consisted of four yoke of cattle, none over four years of age. . . .

May 7—Tonight we camped at Fort Kearny. The fort is built from the land . . . sod and adobe. They tell us the earth walls are warm in the winter and cool in the summer, but they don't hold out the rain. We fixed our wagons as well as we could, and stocked up on flour and bacon. The road ahead follows the Platte River and the next military outpost is Fort Laramie some 300 miles away. . . .

May 19—A wagon fell off the ferry while crossing the river today, rolling and bobbing as the current carried it away. Finally, it brought up on a sand bar. None that witnessed the accident believed it possible that either of the occupants could be found alive, but, to the great surprise and joy of all, the young man extricated himself from under the contents and then brought his sister alive to the surface.

May 26—More wagon trains on the road now. It is quite amusing to note the different mottos on the wagon covers, such as, "From Danville, Ill., and bound for Oregon," or "Bound for California or Bust". . . .

June 12—We came fifteen miles today and camped at Ash Hollow. The road today has been exceedingly rough; scarcely a foot of anything like a level road. . . . This afternoon I saw our first buffalo. Some emigrants, some afoot and

Chimney Rock in western Nebraska was a well-known landmark along the Oregon Trail.

others on horseback, were in hot pursuit. We heard several shots fired, but they did not bring him down. Both buffalo and men very soon passed out of sight beyond the hills. . . .

June 16—We came in view of Courthouse Rock and Chimney Rock about noon today while crossing the ruins of the "ancient bluffs." We have a splendid view of those noted rocks from our camp tonight. . . .

June 18—We started at 6 A.M. and came twelve miles and stopped for lunch near Scott's Bluffs on the Platte River. It commenced raining and blowing a perfect hurricane and we were obliged to form a corral with our wagons for the purpose of preventing a stampede of cattle. The storm had spent its force in about twenty-five minutes without any damage being done. Grazing is very good here, but could find no "buffalo chips" for fuel. . . .

June 22—We passed Fort Laramie yesterday and obtained several little articles needed in camp. . . .

## THE KANSAS-NEBRASKA ACT

As pioneers such as Enoch Conyers were traveling west through the Platte Valley, an increasing number of Americans were becoming interested in making the Great Plains part of the United States. The most important reasons centered around the Platte Valley's importance to overland travel.

Oregon, a destination of many pioneers, was claimed by both the United States and Great Britain. If a United States territory were established in the Great Plains and Rocky Mountains regions, Americans would be able to settle closer to the disputed Oregon land. The presence of significant numbers of settlers in American lands close to the Oregon territory would strengthen the United States' claim to the West Coast lands. Moreover, interest in building a transcontinental railroad, a speedy way to cross the continent to the Pacific, was increasing. Concerns such as these pressured government officials to make Nebraska and the surrounding areas official United States territories.

From the 1830s to the 1860s, a series of treaties was made between the United States government and various Nebraska Indian tribes. These treaties eroded the Indians' claims to the vast lands of Nebraska and allowed the United States to expand its western land holdings. Political pressure to make Nebraska an American territory continued to build.

In 1843, Lieutenant John C. Frémont explored the region and suggested that it be named Nebraska, a name the Oto Indians and many whites had used for the Platte River. The same year, a young politician from Illinois, Stephen A. Douglas, was elected to the United States House of Representatives.

Douglas championed the idea of American expansion west and was particularly enthusiastic about the transcontinental railroad.

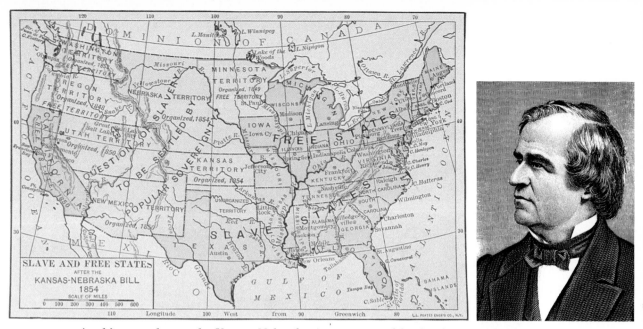

As this map shows, the Kansas-Nebraska Act, sponsored by Stephen Douglas (right), created Kansas and Nebraska as territories in which the question of slavery would be left up to the populace.

In 1844, adopting Frémont's suggestion that the area be called Nebraska, Douglas introduced a bill in the House to organize the Nebraska Territory. However, the bill failed to pass. Douglas was elected to the Senate in 1847, and in 1848 again introduced a bill to organize the territory. However, that too failed, as did another attempt in 1852.

The difficulties Douglas faced in attempting to establish Nebraska as a territory were due largely to the debates over slavery and states' rights that were raging at the time. The northern states wanted to prohibit slavery in any new territories or states being added to the Union. The southern states wanted new territories and states to allow slavery.

In 1854, after many heated debates, Congress passed the Kansas-Nebraska Act, sponsored by Douglas. The bill created two new American territories, Kansas and Nebraska, and gave the people living in each territory the right to decide whether or not the territory would allow slavery.

In the 1850s, most of those who decided to stay in Nebraska settled along the Missouri River.

## NEBRASKA TERRITORY

Nebraska Territory was much larger than the present-day state of Nebraska. It extended from the Missouri River west to the Rocky Mountains, and included parts of present-day Colorado, Montana, North Dakota, South Dakota, and Wyoming. The creation of new territories in 1861 and 1863 reduced Nebraska Territory to a region closely matching the state's present boundaries. (The area that is now Boyd County north of the Niobrara River was annexed in 1890.)

The first governor of Nebraska Territory, Francis Burt, died two days after taking office. Thomas B. Cuming became acting governor and began organizing the territorial government. One of

Cuming's first steps was to order a census. The 1854 census showed that Nebraska's white population was extremely small— only 2,732 people. The territory's Indian population was not included in the census. Most of the white people lived along the Missouri River; a few others lived along the Platte. The rest of the state was virtually devoid of white settlers.

The territorial legislature first met in Omaha on January 16, 1855, less than one year after the tiny settlement had been laid out. The selection of Omaha as territorial capital touched off a feud between it and other developing towns, particularly those in the South Platte River region.

Much of the legislature's early work involved establishing schools and banks. The new territorial banks set up by the legislature soon ran into difficulties. As settlers began arriving in greater numbers, land speculation increased. Speculators borrowed heavily from banks to purchase land that they hoped would soon increase in value. When the banks tried to collect on the loans, the speculators could not pay, and the banks were left without funds. Money to pay for new land and businesses became scarce. A financial panic in 1857 caused all but one of the new banks to fail. Many speculators and settlers lost all their money.

By the time Nebraska Territory was formed, many of the Indian tribes in eastern Nebraska had ceded their lands to the government. However, the more nomadic tribes in the western part of the state continued to contest the growing white encroachment. The Horse Creek Treaty of 1851 reserved as Sioux territory a large area north and west of the fork formed by the North Platte and South Platte rivers. Despite the agreement, occasional violence broke out between the Sioux and the settlers. General William S. Harney and an army of six hundred defeated the Sioux at Ash Hollow along the Platte on September 4, 1855.

In the 1850s and 1860s, the continuing encroachment of white settlers onto Indian lands led to a number of skirmishes between Indians and whites in Nebraska.

In 1859, six Pawnee warriors attacked some settlers in the northeast part of the state. Later that year, General John Thayer and a group of two hundred soldiers surprised a group of Pawnees encamped about ten miles (sixteen kilometers) west of Norfolk. Knowing that there was little chance of defeating the larger military forces, the Pawnees decided to surrender, agreeing to give up the six warriors who had attacked the settlers. They also agreed to pay for damages and to march overland, in the company of American soldiers, to a new home along the Loup River. Periodic conflicts between the Indians and whites continued for a number of years.

Settlers continued to flock to Nebraska. In little more than five years, the population of Nebraska increased tenfold, to 28,841 in 1860. The population would continue to increase sharply. As part of the continuing effort to strengthen its claim on the Oregon territory, the government devised a plan to lure greater numbers of permanent residents to Nebraska Territory.

**A family in front of their sod house in Custer County in 1890**

## THE HOMESTEAD ACT AND THE UNION PACIFIC RAILROAD

In 1862, Congress passed the Free Homestead Act. The act offered 160 acres (65 hectares) of land on the American frontier to any settler willing to farm it. Many thousands of pioneers rushed to Nebraska to claim free land under the new law. However, newcomers to the prairie sometimes found that there were not enough trees in the area with which to build wooden houses. Borrowing a trick from the Indians, they built their houses out of sod (a layer of soil with a thick growth of grass and weeds). When the sod was cut into blocks, it could be used to form walls and roofs.

Construction of the Union Pacific Railroad in the 1860s encouraged settlement of Nebraska.

The shortage of wood also affected the Union Pacific Railroad, which began building the eastern link of the transcontinental railroad in 1865. From its starting point at Omaha, the railroad had to be built westward over 600 miles (966 kilometers) of virtually treeless land. Huge amounts of timber were needed for the railroad ties. Throughout 1864 and 1865, tie-cutting crews scoured long stretches of the Missouri Valley, cutting down every tree large enough to be sawed into railroad ties. Eventually, ties were brought in from as far away as New York State. This railroad that was quickly being built along the Platte Valley would make travel and shipment of goods considerably easier and faster. Consequently, the railroad offered yet another incentive for people to settle in Nebraska.

## THE STRUGGLE TO BECOME THE THIRTY-SEVENTH STATE

The fast-growing population of Nebraska Territory seemed relatively unimpressed by the prospect of statehood. Territorial ballots in 1860 contained a proposition to form a state, but Nebraska voters turned it down. Although a convention to write a state constitution was elected in 1864, it failed to take any action. Finally, in 1866, the territorial legislature created a constitution and presented it to Nebraska voters. Although the proposed constitution was approved, the vote was not overwhelming. There were 7,766 ballots cast, and the constitution passed by a margin of only 100 votes.

A few obstacles to achieving statehood still remained. Congress objected to the provision in the Nebraska constitution that granted the vote only to white males. To gain congressional approval for the state constitution, the Nebraska legislature passed a bill ensuring that black males would be eligible to vote as well.

Finally, in late 1866, Congress passed a bill declaring Nebraska the thirty-seventh state of the United States. President Andrew Johnson, however, vetoed the bill. At the time, a move was being made, primarily by Republican senators, to impeach President Johnson. The senators from the would-be state of Nebraska were Republicans, and the president did not want them to be able to join the fight against him. The struggle finally came to an end early in 1867, when Congress overrode President Johnson's veto. Nebraska was admitted to the Union on March 1, 1867.

# Chapter 7
# A LAND TRANSFORMED

# A LAND TRANSFORMED

The state of Nebraska proved to be as feisty as Nebraska Territory had been. During the first session of the Nebraska legislature, the legislators rekindled the feud over the location of the capital. They voted to move the state capital from Omaha to Lancaster, a tiny town surrounded by prairie. They renamed the town Lincoln.

The state's first governor, Republican David Butler, took office after defeating Democrat Julius Sterling Morton, who had served as acting governor during the state's territorial days. Although Morton lost the election, he actually achieved more lasting fame than the winner. However, his greatest influence in the state proved to be ecological rather than political. Morton realized that adding trees to Nebraska's land would make it more fertile and help it to conserve moisture. For years, he had been planting trees on his property along the Missouri River, and he encouraged others to do the same. In 1872, Morton convinced the state board of agriculture to set aside April 10 as Arbor Day—a day to plant trees on the treeless plains of Nebraska. In 1885, Arbor Day became a legal holiday in Nebraska, and the date was changed to April 22, Morton's birthday. Arbor Day is now celebrated throughout much of the nation, although the date varies from state to state.

## TROUBLE ON THE PLAINS

In 1867, Union Pacific Railroad workers completed laying tracks across the state. But even before the railroad stretched across the plains toward the Rocky Mountains, the Indians of western Nebraska had begun to realize that the settlers and their iron rails threatened their nomadic way of life.

The first of a series of Indian uprisings in the Platte Valley occurred in August 1864. The conflicts escalated as the railroad neared completion. Various tribes began cooperating more closely with each other than ever before. Indians attacked stagecoaches heading west from the Platte Valley to Salt Lake City, causing service to be stopped for a time. The Indians also tore down telegraph wires throughout the valley and ripped up long sections of railroad track.

In August 1867, a party of Cheyenne warriors used torn-down telegraph wire to tie a blockade to the railroad tracks. A handcar carrying six repairmen crashed into the blockade, and the Cheyennes killed five of the men immediately. The sixth, an Englishman named William Thompson, managed to survive even though he had been scalped. By the 1880s, more serious confrontations between whites and Indians had occurred. Many of the Plains Indians were killed in battle. Others died from diseases brought by the white settlers. The survivors were moved to reservations in the more remote areas of Nebraska and in the western territories.

During the last years of the nineteenth century, Nebraskans suffered through several unusually cold winters. Between 1874 and 1877, farmers on the plains were plagued by horrible attacks of grasshoppers. Witnesses to the attacks reported that at times, the huge swarms of grasshoppers formed a gray cloud that

This 1875 engraving shows a family on the plains clearing away the
destruction left behind by an attack of grasshoppers.

extended as far as the eye could see. Descending on the crops, the
insects would devour every plant in sight. In 1890, a severe
drought completely destroyed the crops of many Nebraska
farmers.

Many Nebraska homesteaders, discouraged by the economic
disaster brought on by the droughts and insects, left the plains.
Painted on the side of some of the covered wagons carrying
people out of Nebraska were such laments as WIPED OUT BY
GRASSHOPPERS.

# THE POPULIST MOVEMENT

Nebraska farmers had suffered through one setback after another: declining prices for their crops, harsh winters, droughts, foreclosures. Through all of this, the railroads prospered. The railroad made the land of the Platte Valley more valuable than it had been before. In fact, when the railroad was completed, a number of towns on the plains were moved—literally—to be closer to it. The townspeople would actually tear down a few of the larger buildings and rebuild them near the tracks. A number of "overnight" railroad boomtowns sprang up in this way.

During this time, farmers were dependent on the railroad to ship farm products to eastern markets. Although the farmers were enduring economic setbacks, the railroads were prospering, and the rates for shipping the farm products increased. Many farmers felt that the railroads were getting rich at the expense of the farmer. During the 1870s and 1880s, many of the farmers banded together by joining such groups as the National Grange and the Farmers' Alliance. These organizations sought to influence national and state governmental agencies to make agricultural policies and railroad legislation that would help farmers.

In 1890, a political organization known as the People's party was created. The members of this party were known as Populists. One goal of the Populists was to increase farm-product prices. The Populists suggested that the government increase the amount of money available by minting large amounts of silver coins and paper money. They reasoned that these monetary policies would increase inflation and allow farmers to charge more for their crops. The Populists also believed that stronger laws were needed to regulate the railroads.

The Issue — 1900
·LIBERTY·
·JUSTICE·
·HUMANITY·
W.J. BRYAN
NO CROWN OF THORNS
NO CROSS OF GOLD
EQUAL RIGHTS TO ALL  SPECIAL PRIVILEGES TO NONE.

Nebraska congressman and noted orator William Jennings Bryan, shown here on a 1900 presidential campaign poster, made three unsuccessful bids for the presidency.

William Jennings Bryan, an Illinois lawyer who moved to Nebraska and was elected to the United States House of Representatives, became the Populist movement's most important leader. By 1896, the Populist movement was so strong that both the Populist party and the Democratic party nominated Bryan for president of the United States. Bryan narrowly lost the election. Four years later, he again became the presidential nominee of both parties, and again lost. After 1900, the Populist movement declined.

The Populist party no longer exists, but many major Populist goals, including the development of silver and paper money, were gradually achieved. William Jennings Bryan founded a newspaper

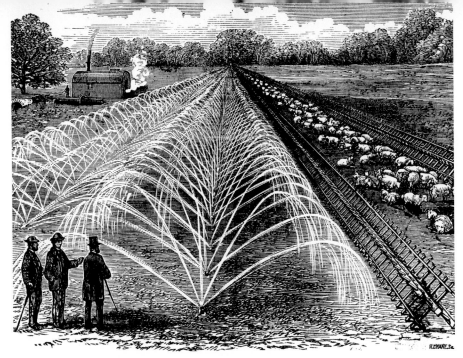

Irrigation of the
plains in the
nineteenth century

in Lincoln, Nebraska, made a third unsuccessful bid for the
presidency in 1908, and eventually became secretary of state
under President Woodrow Wilson.

## GREENING THE PLAINS

Following the extensive drought of the early 1890s, Nebraska
farmers made pioneering steps toward large-scale irrigation of
field crops. These efforts were given a big boost in 1902, when
Congress passed the Reclamation Act, which made federal money
available for irrigation projects. Before long, large parts of the
upper North Platte valley in Scotts Bluff and Morrill counties
were being irrigated, although the problem of distributing water
evenly over large areas persisted for many years.

Northwestern Nebraska was the homesteaders' next challenge.
In 1904, legislation was passed that encouraged people to settle
Nebraska's sparsely populated northwestern region. The Kinkaid
Act offered 640-acre (259-hectare) sites to people willing to farm
the land. Much of the area had been used as open range by cattle

In the twentieth century, Nebraska became the nation's second-largest producer of beef cattle.

ranchers, and parceling the land to homesteaders left little available to ranchers. Although the sites were four times as large as those offered in 1862, the Kinkaid lands were generally unsuitable for farming. Eventually, homesteaders sold their lands to cattle ranchers, who let the lands return to grasses to feed their herds.

During the early years of the twentieth century, agriculture took its place as the cornerstone of the state's economy. Throughout the years of World War I, Nebraska prospered, partly because of increased demand for farm products needed to support the war. Nebraska's cities became centers for food processing and packaging as well as distribution centers for farm products.

In the early 1920s, demand for farm products decreased, prices dropped, and the state's economy suffered the consequences. The extended droughts and dust storms of the 1930s led to desperate conditions. Nearly one-sixth of the population needed assistance from the government to survive. Farmers resorted to threats of physical violence to prevent foreclosures of farm mortgages. In 1933, Governor Charles Bryan enacted a series of farm-mortgage moratorium acts designed to help farmers keep their land.

One of the few bright spots during the era was the discovery of oil in the southeastern part of the state in 1939. A decade later, more oil deposits were discovered in western Nebraska. For several years, petroleum was the state's most important mineral product.

The condition of Nebraska's farm economy improved dramatically during World War II. Wartime food shortages led to record prices for corn, wheat, beef, oats, and potatoes. Unusually plentiful rain, even in the drier areas of the state, led to bumper crops, and prosperity continued.

Nebraska's flat, rolling plains are especially suited for mechanized farming methods. These methods, combined with the productive soil, have helped the state become one of the nation's leaders in farm production. But this growth is not without cost: mechanization is often too expensive for family-owned farms. In Nebraska, as in other states, there has been a trend away from the smaller, family-worked and owned farms, toward larger farms operated by corporations. A state referendum passed in 1982, the Family Farm Preservation Act, limited the purchase of farmland by non-family farm corporations.

## RESOURCE CONTROL

During the twentieth century, modern technology vastly increased the ability of Nebraska farmers to survive spring floods and summer droughts. At the same time, sophisticated irrigation techniques helped make more of Nebraska's land, especially that in the western part of the state, suitable for farming. Together, these factors brought increased agricultural production, as well as new concerns, to Nebraska's farms.

In 1944, an act of Congress created the Missouri River Basin Project (now called the Pick-Sloan Missouri Basin Program). The massive project was designed to control flooding through a series of dams and reservoirs along the Missouri River and many of its tributaries. Dams have been built along a number of Nebraska's rivers, including the Republican, Platte, and Niobrara. The dams help control water levels so that flooding is reduced and water is available during the dry summer months.

By 1950, all of the state's farm and ranch lands were included in the state's soil-conservation programs that had begun in the 1930s. These programs include contour farming, diversification of crops, and range management to prevent overgrazing. These measures have gone far in conserving Nebraska's precious topsoil. The flood-control projects have also aided soil conservation. However, a series of violent spring storms in the early 1980s damaged the soil as well as crops, indicating that additional or more extensive soil-conservation measures are needed.

In the 1960s, a new irrigation device, the self-propelled center-pivot sprinkler, came into general use. This new technology, in which moving sprinklers are carried along water pipes suspended above the ground, enabled farmers to irrigate more land more evenly than ever before. The agricultural advances brought by center-pivot irrigation have dramatically changed the nature of Nebraska agriculture. By 1985, Nebraska ranked among the top three irrigated states in the nation, with nearly 8 million acres (3.2 million hectares) of irrigated land. Irrigation has reduced the damage created by droughts and has helped Nebraska farmers stabilize their crop production.

The self-propelled center-pivot sprinkler, which came into general use in the 1960s, enabled Nebraska farmers to irrigate more land more evenly than ever before.

Although modern advances in irrigation have helped foster productive farms on previously unsuitable land, these advances have also created new problems. Irrigation in the nineteenth and early twentieth centuries was based on directing the flow of river and stream water through ditch canals. Today's methods, which require more water, entail pumping water from the state's groundwater reserves. Nearly three-fourths of Nebraska's irrigated lands use water pumped from wells. This has lessened the amount of underground water available in many areas and has led to some contamination of groundwater as well. The extensive use of modern irrigation techniques in the eastern Sand Hills region has upset that area's fragile ecology. In some places, dunes once covered by a variety of grasses are now barren and eroded.

Nebraskans, ever mindful of the importance of their land, are keeping a watchful eye on their resources. The state that has survived droughts, insect infestations, and economic depression will surely find a way to keep its resources protected and its lands productive.

# Chapter 8

# GOVERNMENT
# AND THE ECONOMY

# GOVERNMENT AND THE ECONOMY

"We created history here in Nebraska," said Governor-elect Kay Orr on the NBC "Today" show the morning after her victory in the November 1986 election. History was indeed made in Nebraska as Kay Orr became the first female Republican governor in United States history. However, Orr and her Democratic challenger, Helen Boosalis, were making history long before the November 5 election. Their gubernatorial race was the first in American history in which the candidates of both major political parties were women. The 1986 Nebraska gubernatorial election was a notably progressive one—dispelling many people's mistaken belief that Nebraska is a staid and conservative state.

## NEBRASKA'S UNIQUE LEGISLATURE

Every state in the nation has a legislature made up of two houses patterned after those of the United States Congress—every state, that is, except Nebraska. Until 1937, Nebraska's legislature was organized like that of the other states. In 1934, however, George Norris, a United States senator from Nebraska, began to campaign for change.

Norris argued that the bicameral (two-house) legislature was outdated. He suggested that the upper and lower houses were little more than unnecessary customs based on the English class system, which he felt had no place in a democracy. Norris led the

**The state capitol in Lincoln**

movement to place a proposition on the Nebraska election ballot to form a unicameral (one-house) legislature.

Norris also objected to a primary feature of bicameral legislatures: conference committees. These committees are staffed by senators and representatives to work out differences in similar bills passed by both houses. The committees usually meet in "closed" sessions; no public record of the deals and compromises is made. Senator Norris argued that these closed meetings had no place in democratic government.

Some Nebraskans had been discussing the idea of a unicameral legislature for years. Norris's plan, however, was more radical than previous proposals. He suggested that the politicians in the legislature be made nonpartisan, meaning they would be responsible only to the people of their electoral districts rather than to the views of a particular political party.

The unicameral legislature proposal was put on the election ballot in 1934, at the height of the Great Depression. The economic climate highlighted a practical aspect of the senator's idea: a legislature consisting of one house would need fewer legislators. The number of government officials would be reduced, saving the state a considerable amount of money. The voters of eighty-four of the state's ninety-three counties approved the measure, and Nebraska's innovative unicameral legislature met for the first time in January of 1937. Now more than half a century old, it is considered by many to be a model of efficiency.

Until 1964, each representative from the state's forty-nine legislative districts was elected to a two-year term. Since then, the legislators have been elected to four-year terms. The legislature meets once a year, but special sessions may be called by the governor.

## THE USUAL AND UNUSUAL IN NEBRASKA GOVERNMENT

The fundamental laws of Nebraska are framed in a state constitution adopted in 1875, which replaced the earlier constitution of 1866. Amendments to the constitution may be proposed in the legislature or by the voters of Nebraska. An amendment may be adopted only after it has been approved by a majority of Nebraska's voters, and, if initiated by the legislature, by three-fifths of the legislature as well.

Nebraska's governor serves a four-year term, and may serve no more than two terms in a row. The state treasurer, like the governor, may serve only two terms in succession. Most of the other top officials in the executive branch of government are permitted to serve an unlimited number of four-year terms.

Nebraska's judicial system is headed by a supreme court

composed of a chief justice and six associate justices. The lower courts are district and county courts. Nebraska judges, unlike those in many other states, are elected on a nonpartisan basis.

Elections for some county and local government officials are also nonpartisan, giving the state's elections a unique character. Another unusual characteristic of Nebraska state government is that the constitution prohibits state-bonded indebtedness. This means that government officials cannot borrow money to fund state programs. For a state considered by many to be conservative and traditional, Nebraska presents a wealth of surprises.

## REVENUE

The property tax levied as part of the state's 1875 constitution was repealed in 1966. In 1967, Nebraska turned to a general sales tax and a personal income tax to generate state revenue. The state's annual income is about $1.5 billion. More than 25 percent of this income comes from the federal government in the form of various programs; the rest comes from state taxes.

The state's annual expenditures are also about $1.5 billion. Education is Nebraska's greatest expenditure, using about one-third of the state's revenue. Other major expenditures include highways and public welfare.

## EDUCATION

From the earliest pioneer days, education has played a part in the daily lives of Nebraskans. The first schools were established by missionaries who wanted to teach Christianity to the Indians. The United States Army established the region's first school for white children at Fort Atkinson in 1820. Throughout the 1830s and

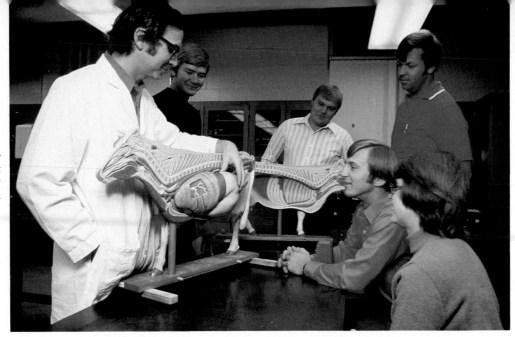

An agriculture
class at
the University
of Nebraska

1840s, most students were taught by church groups and private
tutors. The first free school was established in 1855, one year after
Nebraska became a territory. Compulsory attendance for students
between the ages of seven and fifteen has been required by state
law since 1891.

About 267,000 students are enrolled in Nebraska's public
elementary and secondary schools. The state spends nearly $3,500
per student every year. Private elementary schools have an
enrollment of about 21,000 students; about 27,000 students attend
private high schools. The state has several special schools for
handicapped students.

Nebraska offers many opportunities for higher education. Peru
State College was chartered when Nebraska was a territory,
making it the oldest college in the state. The University of
Nebraska, chartered in 1869 and opened in 1871, was the first
land-grant college west of the Mississippi River. The university
has approximately 25,000 students enrolled at the Lincoln campus
and about 14,000 at the Omaha campus. In addition, about 2,500
medical students attend the university's medical school in Omaha.

Corn (inset), much of which is ground into feed for livestock (above),
is Nebraska's chief crop.

Other major universities and colleges are located in Omaha,
Lincoln, Bellevue, Hastings, Fremont, Wayne, Kearney, Crete,
Blair, and Seward.

## AGRICULTURE

During the nineteenth century, the majority of Nebraska's
residents lived or worked on farms and ranches. In the 1980s,
about 13 percent of the state's work force was employed directly
in agriculture. Farm products account for about 11 percent of the
state's economic output. The goods produced by Nebraska's farms
and ranches are enjoyed throughout the nation. The state ranks
sixth in the nation in total farm sales.

Sugar beets are an important crop in western Nebraska.

Nebraska farmers produce about 10 percent of the nation's corn. Corn, a crop that requires a large amount of water, is raised extensively in the eastern regions of the state and in the intensively irrigated sections of central Nebraska. Much of the corn grown in Nebraska is feed corn for the state's livestock. Nebraska traditionally ranks first or second in the nation in the production of popcorn.

Other major crops grown in the eastern third of the state are soybeans, wheat, oats, sorghum (a feed grain), and alfalfa. The farmers of western Nebraska raise winter wheat, beans, sugar beets, potatoes, and rye.

Nebraska is the nation's second-largest supplier of beef cattle and calves. Cattle are the state's most important farm product, providing 40 percent of the state's agricultural income. Most of Nebraska's cattle are raised in the Sand Hills and in the western part of the state.

Livestock and livestock products, including hogs (left) and poultry
(right), account for 60 percent of Nebraska's agricultural income.

Hog farms can be found in every one of the state's ninety-three
counties. Nebraska ranks sixth in the nation in pork production.
The state also has a large number of dairy farms, poultry farms,
and sheep ranches. Bees raised by Nebraska farmers produce
between 5 million and 10 million pounds (2.3 million and 4.5
million kilograms) of honey each year. Bees are also integral to
alfalfa production because they pollinate the alfalfa flowers.

## GOODS

Manufacturing and light industry account for about 19 percent
of the state's income. Food processing is the state's largest
industry. Processed foods, produced throughout the state, include

**Beef cattle, raised mainly in the Sand Hills and in the western part of the state, are Nebraska's single most-important farm product.**

dairy products such as butter and ice cream, canned vegetables, flour, and sugar. Omaha is a center of the nation's meat-packing industry.

More than half of the state's industry is concentrated in the cities of Lincoln and Omaha. Nebraska has worked to develop an economy that will withstand such agricultural uncertainties as failing crops or falling prices. Between 1964 and 1984, the number of people employed in industry in Nebraska increased by 50 percent. As workers leave the farms, the state must continue to expand its manufacturing and industry. However, the state has few raw materials with which to support heavy industry. Instead, it must turn to the manufacture of items that require technical sophistication but only small amounts of raw materials.

Nebraska is a leading insurance center. Mutual of Omaha, the nation's largest health-insurance company, is based in Omaha.

## SERVICES

Service industries provide the largest portion, 70 percent, of Nebraska's income. These industries, which include government, employ about two-thirds of the state's work force and are concentrated in Lincoln, Omaha, and near Sioux City, Iowa. Finance, insurance, and real estate are significant service industries, providing about 16 percent of the state's income. Mutual of Omaha, the world's largest health-insurance company, has its headquarters in Omaha. Lincoln, the center of the state's government, is also an insurance center and a leading wholesale and retail trade center.

The condition of service industries in Nebraska is tied to the condition of agriculture. If corn or cattle production decreases, the transportation and wholesale trade services for farm products are affected. If prices for farm products decline, farmers have less money to spend on retail goods, fewer retail clerks are needed, and fewer goods need to be manufactured. Therefore, Nebraskans continue to staunchly support the farmers while seeking ways to expand their state's economy.

Chapter 9

# ARTS AND LEISURE

# ARTS AND LEISURE

In Nebraska, unusual forms of entertainment are often the rule. Although the state has no major-league professional sports teams and few world-famous musical and dramatic groups, it still holds its share of surprises. Some people who move from urban areas to the remote plains of Nebraska complain about the lack of cultural centers away from the state's major cities. But Nebraska's plains have produced several of America's most accomplished writers.

## THREE FAMOUS WRITERS

Willa Cather was perhaps the most famous writer to be associated with Nebraska. Born in Virginia in 1873, she moved with her family to Nebraska at the age of ten, and graduated from the University of Nebraska in 1895. *O Pioneers!*, published in 1913, was the first of many books in which Cather portrayed pioneer life on the Nebraska frontier. Her novel *One of Ours*, about a Nebraska farmer who dies in World War I, won the 1923 Pulitzer Prize in fiction. Other noted works by Cather set in Nebraska include *My Antonia* and *A Lost Lady*.

Mari Sandoz was born in the Nebraska Sand Hills country during the homestead period and was educated at the University of Nebraska. Her father, Jules Sandoz, was a friend of the Sioux and Cheyenne Indians of north-central Nebraska. He became the subject of *Old Jules*, one of her famous nonfiction works. Sandoz wrote many other books about pioneer life on the Great Plains, including *The Beaver Men, Crazy Horse, Cheyenne Autumn,* and *The Buffalo Hunters,* as well as a number of novels and a collection of shorter works. Speaking about her life on the plains, she once said, "We were taught a wonderful at-homeness in the world and the universe. We learned the meaning of every change in sky and earth. . . . Have you ever heard a prairie song lark rise into the clear, thin air of the High Plains, spilling song golden as sunlight around him?"

John G. Neihardt was another well-known Nebraska writer. One of his most famous books, *Black Elk Speaks,* is the record of an interview Neihardt conducted with an aged Oglala Sioux holy man. Black Elk described many memories, including the last Sioux uprising and the Sioux's defeat at the hands of the American soldiers. Although Neihardt was born in Illinois, he lived for many years in Nebraska, first in Wayne, and then in Bancroft near the Omaha Indian Reservation. Five of his epic poems about frontier life were collected into one large volume called *A Cycle of the West.* In 1921, an act by the state legislature named him poet laureate of Nebraska. In 1923, he was appointed professor of poetry at the University of Nebraska.

Although none of these noted writers is still alive, their works live on. Nebraska continues to honor these authors with formal memorials: the Willa Cather Historical Center, located in Red Cloud; the Mari Sandoz Museum, in Gordon; and the Neihardt Center, in Bancroft.

## CULTURAL EVENTS

Nebraska offers many opportunities for lovers of music, theater, and dance. In Omaha, the Orpheum Theater is home of Omaha's symphony orchestra, opera, and ballet. Many other musical artists

The Sheldon Gallery
in Lincoln (above) and
the Joslyn Art Museum
in Omaha (right) house
fine art collections.

and groups, including road companies of Broadway shows, perform at the Orpheum. The Nebraska State Repertory Company presents stage plays year-round at the Rudyard Norton Theater in Omaha. A number of other theaters and stage companies are active in and around Omaha as well.

Other theatrical productions, some associated with the University of Nebraska, are presented in Lincoln. The oldest repertory company in the state, run by Nebraska Wesleyan University, performs every summer at the Village Theater in Brownville.

A number of exhibits are presented each year at the well-known Joslyn Art Museum in Omaha and the Sheldon Gallery of the University of Nebraska at Lincoln. Many other historical and natural-history museums are scattered throughout the state.

## OUTDOOR RECREATION

Nebraska has sixty-six state recreation areas encompassing more than 111,000 acres (44,922 hectares). Most of them enable

Chadron State Park in the Pine Ridge is one of six beautiful state parks in Nebraska.

visitors to enjoy such outdoor activities as swimming, camping, boating, fishing, hunting, bicycling, cross-country skiing, snowmobiling, and horseback riding.

One of the state's most unusual recreation areas is the Nebraska National Forest, established in 1902 to prove that it was possible to successfully plant trees in the Sand Hills region. All of the trees of the Bessey division of the forest, in Thomas and Blain counties, were planted. A disastrous fire destroyed much of the Bessey division in 1965, and much of it is now being reforested. The Pine Ridge division of the Nebraska National Forest lies in Dawes and Sioux counties in the northwest part of the state. McKelvie National Forest, in north-central Nebraska, is part natural forest and part planted forest.

The Buffalo Bill Rodeo is held during Nebraskaland Days, an annual, week-long celebration that takes place near North Platte.

## NEBRASKA'S EXCITING RODEOS

Modern-day cowboys still roam the ranges of western and north-central Nebraska, and rodeos, both large and small, remain popular summertime events. The Buffalo Bill Rodeo, held in June as part of Nebraskaland Days near the town of North Platte, is one of the state's most famous showcases for cowboy talent.

Professional rodeo riders also compete for top prizes in Nebraska's Biggest Rodeo in Burwell, and in Omaha's Ak-Sar-Ben Rodeo. Dozens of other county and community rodeos are held throughout the state, and most county fairs in western Nebraska feature plenty of rodeo action.

## WHERE COLLEGE ATHLETICS REIGN SUPREME

What Nebraska lacks in major-league professional sports, it more than makes up for in big-time college athletics. Every spring, Omaha plays host to the National Collegiate Athletic Association's World Series baseball games. Although these games

**Nebraska football fans passionately follow the exploits of the University of Nebraska Cornhuskers.**

create considerable interest, even more excitement is generated by the start of the fall football season.

At every football game at the University of Nebraska's Memorial Stadium in Lincoln, some seventy thousand loyal fans can be heard yelling "Go Big Red!" as if with a single voice. The Cornhuskers are a perpetual powerhouse in college football. In the past decade, they have finished most of their seasons as one of the top ten teams in the nation. Throughout the 1980s, they battled their arch rivals, the Oklahoma Sooners, for the Big Eight Conference Championship.

Nebraska fans give the word *loyalty* a new dimension. Season tickets to Cornhusker games are frequently willed to family members. Bitter "custody" battles over cherished season tickets have been known to occur in some Nebraska divorce cases. Some fans even claim to have mortgaged their homes and businesses in order to raise the money needed to follow the team on the road.

Chapter 10

# HIGHLIGHTS OF THE CORNHUSKER STATE

# HIGHLIGHTS OF THE CORNHUSKER STATE

To millions who have traveled through the Platte Valley—from the days of covered wagons to the era of superhighways—Nebraska may have appeared flat and featureless. The historic route along the Platte was chosen for convenience, not scenery. Those who take a more careful look, however, will find that the Nebraska landscape reveals a number of pleasant surprises for the traveler.

## OMAHA AND THE MISSOURI VALLEY

Several landmarks and sites near Omaha are world famous. In 1917, a Roman Catholic priest named Edward Flanagan founded a school and home for neglected and troubled youths that eventually came to be called Boys Town. Father Flanagan's careful work, based on his philosophy that "there is no such thing as a bad boy," helped thousands of boys to grow up and lead productive lives, and Boys Town soon achieved worldwide recognition. Today the campus, located about ten miles (sixteen kilometers) west of Omaha, provides a home for about four hundred girls and boys.

Just south of Omaha along the Missouri River is the historic town of Bellevue, site of the first permanent white settlement in Nebraska. A number of mid-nineteenth-century buildings have been restored and are on display. One such building is the Fontenelle Bank, Nebraska's first bank, which opened in 1855 and

closed two years later during the financial panic of 1857. The oldest structure on display in Bellevue is a settler's cabin that was probably built around 1830.

The headquarters of the Strategic Air Command (SAC) is located at Offutt Air Force Base just south of Bellevue. Near SAC headquarters is the Strategic Air Command Museum, where visitors can see a five-screen reenactment of a SAC "red alert," as well as a wide variety of airplanes and guided missiles.

The Joslyn Art Museum in Omaha houses a fine collection of art from all over the world, including a special exhibit of art by and about American Indians of the 1800s. The Omaha Children's Museum has hands-on exhibits that help youngsters learn about science and nature. More than a thousand species of animals from around the world are featured in lifelike habitats at Omaha's Henry Doorly Zoo. The Great Plains Black History Museum claims to have the most complete exhibit of black history west of the Mississippi River. The Mormon Pioneer Cemetery marks the final resting place of nearly six hundred Mormon pioneers who died while traveling westward during the bitter winter of 1846-47.

Aircraft at the Strategic Air Command Museum in Bellevue

Shoppers who want to take a nostalgic trip back to the Omaha of the early 1900s can walk down the brick streets of the Old Market area of the city. Those interested in the day-to-day activity of a modern livestock market can visit the Omaha Stockyards and Livestock Market. On a busy day, more than six thousand head of cattle are housed in the state's only commercial stockyard.

Rosenblatt Stadium is the home of the College World Series and the Omaha Royals, a class AAA farm affiliate of the Kansas City Royals baseball team. The largest amusement park in Nebraska is Omaha's Peony Park, which features thrill rides, miniature golf, and a sandy beach, as well as many other attractions. Sunset Speedway hosts auto races on Sunday nights from Memorial Day to Labor Day.

One of Omaha's most popular tourist attractions is the Union Pacific Historical Museum, which features fascinating railroad

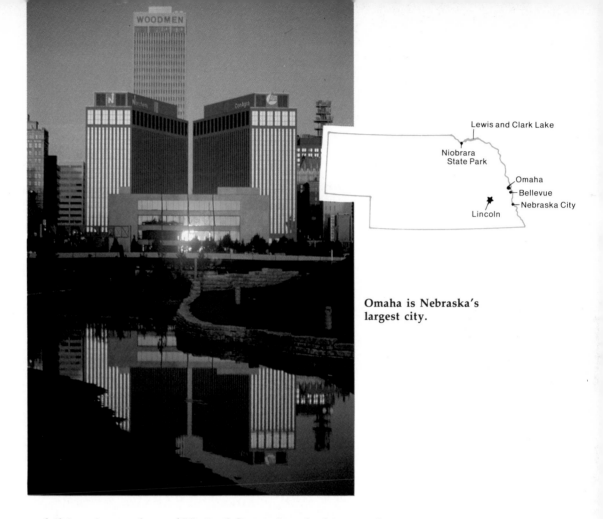

Omaha is Nebraska's largest city.

exhibits. A number of United States battleships and even a submarine can be seen at Freedom Park, located in the Greater Omaha Marina along the Missouri River.

Omaha was the birthplace of Gerald R. Ford, the thirty-eighth president of the United States. Ford moved to Michigan with his mother when he was about two years old. A garden and monument at his birthsite are open to the public.

Much of the Missouri Valley north of Omaha is famous for its spectacular scenery. Nebraskans who love the outdoors flock to Ponca State Park, Lewis and Clark Lake, and Niobrara State Park.

South of Omaha, along the Missouri River, is Nebraska City. Here, the carefully preserved mansion of J. Sterling Morton,

Arbor House in Nebraska City (above) was the home
of Arbor Day founder J. Sterling Morton.
The domed tower of the state capitol in Lincoln
(right) can be seen for miles.

founder of Arbor Day, is the centerpiece of Arbor Lodge State
Historical Park and Tree Trail. Autumn automobile tours through
Morton's apple orchards are popular with area residents and
visitors alike.

## LINCOLN, CAPITAL OF NEBRASKA

Those who travel to Lincoln cannot miss seeing the 400-foot
(122-meter) domed tower of the state capitol, visible for miles.
Built between 1922 and 1932 at a cost of nearly $10 million, the
building has long been considered a masterpiece. When
construction was started in 1922, the new structure was built in
sections around the existing capitol. This was done so that

government employees could continue working in their old offices until new ones were completed.

In a number of larger rooms inside the elegant building are large paintings and mosaics depicting Nebraska history. Some of the most spectacular are the six mosaic murals that were added to the Great Hall in 1967. Former Nebraska governor Robert Kerrey wrote of the capitol that it "reflects the spirit of the brave pioneers who came to Nebraska and the noble people who inhabited this land before them."

Another attraction in Lincoln is the museum housed in Morrill Hall at the University of Nebraska. Nicknamed "Elephant Hall," the museum houses an enormous collection of extinct mammal bones and fossils, including those of the elephantlike mammoths that once roamed the Great Plains. Major art collections are housed at the school's Sheldon Memorial Art Gallery, which features the work of modern American artists; and the Christlieb Western Art Collection. The Nebraska Cornhuskers football team plays its home games at nearby Memorial Stadium.

Also of interest in Lincoln are the elegant governor's mansion, which stands across the street from the capitol; the Nebraska State Historical Society Museum; and the unusual American Historical Society of Germans from Russia, which features exhibits about Germans who settled in Russia before moving to the United States. On Sumner Street is the home of William Jennings Bryan, the "boy orator of the Platte" and three-time presidential candidate.

## THE HISTORIC PLATTE RIVER VALLEY

Travelers on Interstate 80 through the Platte Valley can see many of the same sites the pioneers saw when they headed west in their covered wagons. In Grand Island on the Platte River is the beautiful, modernistic headquarters of the Stuhr Museum of the Prairie Pioneer. The museum maintains a huge display called "Railroad Town" that includes sixty restored buildings and an operating steam train.

A short distance west, near the town of Kearney, is Fort Kearny State Historical Park. The park features a replica of Fort Kearny, one of a chain of forts that was built to protect the wagon trains traveling westward along the Oregon Trail. Among the re-created buildings are a stockade, a blacksmith shop, and lookout towers.

West of Kearney, at Gothenburg, is a beautifully preserved Pony Express station. Farther west, at Maxwell, is lovely Fort McPherson National Cemetery.

Just a few miles west of Maxwell is the historic town of North Platte, Nebraska's fourth-largest city. Once the home of cowboy and showman William "Buffalo Bill" Cody, North Platte was the original site of Cody's extremely successful Wild West Show and Rodeo. For years, Buffalo Bill Cody's show toured much of the United States and even Europe. During Nebraskaland Days in June, much of the excitement of Buffalo Bill's original shows is recaptured in North Platte's rodeos. Free evening rodeos are held throughout the remaining summer months. Buffalo Bill Ranch State Historical Park near North Platte is the site of Scouts Rest Ranch, a house built by Cody in 1878. The huge barn at the ranch was used as the winter home for the Wild West Show troupe.

If, like the pioneers, one follows the North Platte River westward from the town of North Platte, one will see some of western Nebraska's most stirring sites. Courthouse Rock, Jail Rock, Chimney Rock, and Scotts Bluff were among the unusual natural formations that became milestones for the pioneers who

After spending most of the year touring with the Wild West Show (top left), Buffalo Bill and his troupe wintered at Scouts Rest Ranch in North Platte (bottom left).

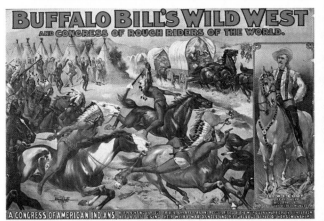

A Pony Express station in Cozad (top right) and ruts left by the wheels of wagon trains (bottom right) are among the reminders of the pioneer era that can still be seen along the route of the historic Oregon Trail.

followed the Oregon and Mormon trails. Courthouse and Jail rocks are virtually unchanged since the pioneers passed by them in covered wagons more than a century ago. Modern visitors can hike along area trails and study a mobile museum display that depicts the history of these landmarks.

A reenactment of
an encampment on
the Oregon Trail
at Scotts Bluff
National Monument

Visitors to Scotts Bluff National Monument can see the deep
ruts formed by the wagon trains that passed the famous
landmark, and tour a museum featuring the paintings and
photographs of pioneer artist William Henry Jackson. For
spectacular views of the western Nebraska countryside, much of it
irrigated farmland, one can drive to the top of Scotts Bluff. The
more adventuresome can hike along Summit Trail, where a series
of numbered posts explain the historic and natural significance of
the area.

## A LAND AS VARIED AS AMERICA

The Sand Hills, in the north-central part of the state, have a
strange, enchanting beauty. In a region with land too dry to farm,
hundreds of small lakes shimmer among sand dunes covered with
golden grasses and native wildflowers. A visitor might see ducks
drifting lazily on the water and perhaps a blackbird winging its
way toward a solitary tree in the distance.

To the west of the Sand Hills, in the northwest corner of the
state, is one of the most fascinating—and isolated—regions of

Nebraska. In this corner, a small part of the Badlands of South Dakota dips into Nebraska.

Surprisingly, this same rugged corner of the state boasts some of the densest forests in Nebraska. Hugging the hills known as the Pine Ridge are thick stands of cedar and pine. Antelope, elk, and deer can be seen wandering through the area.

Even in this wild, rugged land, the stamp of human history has been made. The little town of Crawford in the Pine Ridge area is the site of one of the most famous forts in the history of the American West. Fort Robinson was active as a United States cavalry post between 1874 and 1948. Sioux chief Crazy Horse was killed there by a soldier's bayonet after resisting imprisonment in 1877. Today, visitors can stay in the original barracks and officers' quarters on the fort grounds. Planned activities at the fort include stagecoach and wagon rides, plays, film programs, horseback rides in the picturesque Pine Ridge countryside, chuck-wagon cookouts, and camp-fire sing-alongs. Now a museum and state park, Fort Robinson is one of Nebraska's most popular vacation sites.

Nebraska, once viewed as little more than a highway west, has many secrets to share with its visitors. It was mistakenly called the "Great American Desert" because it seemed flat, sandy, and treeless. But little by little, pioneers, and then settlers, began to discover what the land had to offer. Expanses of Indian hunting grounds that were once roamed by herds of buffalo are now vast grazing ranges that support herds of cattle. Land once thought too dry for crops is now irrigated, yielding in abundance even such moisture-loving crops as corn. What was once a way station on a journey is now a starting place for many of the nation's farm products. Nebraska and its people have made an indelible mark on the nation.

# FACTS AT A GLANCE

## GENERAL INFORMATION

**Statehood:** March 1, 1867, thirty-seventh state

**Origin of Name:** The name Nebraska comes from the Oto Indian word *Nebrathka*, which means "flat water" and was used to describe the Platte River. In 1843, Lieutenant John C. Frémont suggested that the name be used for a territory that included what is now Nebraska.

**State Capital:** Lincoln, founded 1867

**State Nickname:** "Cornhusker State" has been the state's official nickname since 1945. Between 1895 and 1945, the state was called the "Treeplanter's State."

**State Flag:** Nebraska's official state flag, adopted in 1925, features the state seal, imprinted in gold, in the center of a blue field. The flag is fringed with gold on three sides. Around the outer edge of the circular seal are the words "Great Seal of the State of Nebraska" and "March 1st, 1867," the date the state joined the Union. The state motto appears on a printed banner near the top of the seal. The seal also depicts several symbols of Nebraska's pioneer days, including a blacksmith with a hammer and anvil, a settler's cabin with sheaves of wheat and stalks of growing corn, a steamboat sailing on a river, and a steam-powered train heading toward the Rocky Mountains.

**State Motto:** "Equality Before the Law"

**State Bird:** Meadowlark

**State Fossil:** Mammoth

**State Flower:** Goldenrod

**State Tree:** Cottonwood

**State Insect:** Honeybee

**State Rock:** Prairie agate

**Prairie near Red Cloud**

**State Song:** "Beautiful Nebraska," words by Jim Fras and Guy Miller, music by
Jim Fras; adopted as the official state song in 1967:

> Beautiful Nebraska, peaceful prairieland,
> Laced with many rivers and the hills of sand;
> Dark green valleys cradled in the earth,
> Rain and sunshine bring abundant birth.
>
> Beautiful Nebraska, as you look around,
> You will find a rainbow reaching to the ground;
> All these wonders by the Master's hand,
> Beautiful Nebraska land.
>
> We are so proud of this state where we live,
> There is no place that has so much to give.
>
> Beautiful Nebraska, as you look around,
> You will find a rainbow reaching to the ground;
> All these wonders by the Master's hand,
> Beautiful Nebraska land.

# POPULATION

**Population:** 1,569,825, thirty-fifth among the states (1980 census)

**Population Density:** 20.5 people per sq. mi. (8 people per km²)

**Population Distribution:** Although many of Nebraska's farmers have moved to towns and cities, the state is predominantly rural. Three cities in the state have populations of more than 25,000 people. About 31 percent of all Nebraskans live in either Omaha or Lincoln. The remaining 69 percent live on ranches, farms, and in small towns of less than 35,000 people.

| | |
|---|---:|
| Omaha | 313,939 |
| Lincoln | 171,932 |
| Grand Island | 33,180 |
| North Platte | 24,509 |
| Fremont | 23,979 |
| Hastings | 23,045 |
| Bellevue | 21,813 |

(Population figures according to 1980 census)

**Population Growth:** During the second half of the nineteenth century, the population of Nebraska grew rapidly; since 1900, the population has increased more slowly.

| Year | Population |
|---|---:|
| 1854 (territory) | 2,732 |
| 1860 (territory) | 28,841 |
| 1870 | 122,993 |
| 1880 | 452,402 |
| 1890 | 1,062,656 |
| 1900 | 1,066,300 |
| 1910 | 1,192,214 |
| 1920 | 1,296,372 |
| 1930 | 1,377,963 |
| 1940 | 1,315,834 |
| 1950 | 1,325,510 |
| 1960 | 1,417,000 |
| 1970 | 1,483,791 |
| 1980 | 1,569,825 |

# GEOGRAPHY

**Borders:** States that border Nebraska are South Dakota on the north, Iowa and Missouri on the east, Kansas on the south, Colorado on the south and west, and Wyoming on the west.

**The Platte River near Grand Island**

**Highest Point:** 5,426 ft. (1,654 m), in Kimball County in the southwest part of the state

**Lowest Point:** 840 ft. (256 m), in Richardson County near the southeast corner of the state

**Greatest Distances:** North to south—206 mi. (331 km)
East to west—415 mi. (668 km)

**Area:** 77,355 sq. mi. (200,350 km²)

**Rank in Area Among the States:** Fifteenth

**Rivers:** Nebraska has 11,000 mi. (17,703 km) of rivers and streams. All of these rivers and streams eventually empty into the Missouri River, one of the nation's greatest rivers. The Missouri forms the entire eastern boundary and a small portion of the northern boundary of the state. Within Nebraska, the chief tributaries of the Missouri are the Platte and its branches, the Niobrara, the Republican, the Big Blue and the Little Blue, and the Nemaha. The Platte River, which flows through the state from west to east, is a shallow river—occasionally as little as 1 ft. (.3 m) deep—making it unsuitable for navigation. Nevertheless, the Platte and its tributaries are important to the state, together draining more than half of the total land area of the state. The Loup and Elkhorn rivers, which rise in the Sand Hills to the north and flow southeastward, are important tributaries of the Platte.

**Lake McConaughy is Nebraska's largest lake.**

**Lakes:** Most of Nebraska's more than two thousand lakes are small; the larger lakes have been artificially created by damming certain rivers. The largest concentration of naturally occurring lakes is found in the Sand Hills region, which boasts several hundred small, shallow lakes and an even larger number of ponds. Lake McConaughy, created by Kingsley Dam on the North Platte River, is the largest lake in the state, covering about 55 sq. mi. (142 km²). Other large man-made lakes include Lewis and Clark Lake on the Missouri River (approximately half of which lies in South Dakota); Harlan County Lake, Swanson Lake, Enders Reservoir, and Harry Strunk Lake on the Republican River and its tributaries; Box Butte Reservoir on the Niobrara River; and Jeffrey Reservoir, Sutherland Reservoir, and Johnson Lake along the Platte system. These reservoirs and lakes provide recreation for Nebraskans as well as flood control, water for irrigation, and, in some cases, hydroelectric power.

**Topography:** Nebraska is generally described as a series of rolling plateaus that rise from the southeast toward the west at an average incline of 10 ft. per mi. (3 m per km). The land is classified into two major regions: the Great Plains, which cover most of Nebraska and include the Sand Hills, the High Plains, and the Badlands regions; and the Central Lowlands, which cover the eastern fifth of the state.

The land of the Central Lowlands is characterized by a covering of loess, a type of fine dust that is blown about by the wind unless stabilized by vegetation. This loess country covers about 42,000 sq. mi. (108,780 km²) in the eastern third of the state. The gentle, undulating ridges of the loess region, created by water and wind erosion, can support a wide variety of cultivated crops.

The Great Plains of Nebraska are dominated by the Sand Hills region. The Sand Hills region is the largest area of sand hills in the Western Hemisphere, covering more than 20,000 sq. mi. (51,800 km²) in the north-central part of the state. These sand hills are covered with grasses. Although the surface land is dry, the area has numerous lakes and streams and a high water table, making it ideal for cattle ranching. The High Plains, covering about 12,000 sq. mi. (31,080 km²), lie west and northwest of the Sand Hills. This high, generally flat land is in some places cut by deep canyons. Although the area is generally treeless, two small mountain ranges in the region, Wild Cat Ridge and Pine Ridge, support extensive evergreen forests. The small Badlands region covers about 1,000 sq. mi. (2,590 km²) in the extreme northwest corner of the state. This area is an extension of the famous Badlands of neighboring South Dakota.

**Climate:** Nebraska's climate is marked by extreme changes; the state experiences very cold winters and very hot summers. However, within a season, temperatures do not vary widely among different regions of the state. Summer temperatures of over 100° F. (38° C) are common. Three cities have recorded the state's highest temperature of 118° F. (48° C): Geneva, on July 15, 1934; Hartington, on July 17, 1936; and Minden, on July 24, 1936. The coldest temperature ever recorded in the state was -47° F. (-44° C), at Camp Clarke near Northport, on February 12, 1899. In the winter, the state averages ten or more days of temperatures below 0° F. (-18° C). Precipitation varies greatly from west to east. The dry, western portion of Nebraska receives less than 18 in. (46 cm) of rainfall during an average year, while the eastern section of the state receives an average of 27 in. (69 cm). The eastern portion of the state also receives about 30 in. (76 cm) of snowfall a year; the west generally receives somewhat less. Violent storms, including tornadoes, thunderstorms, hailstorms, and blizzards, occur throughout the state. Nebraska averages about ten tornadoes and twenty to twenty-five hailstorms annually.

## NATURE

**Trees:** Only 2 percent of Nebraska's land is forested, and many of these forests were planted; species include green ash, cedar, box elder, cottonwood, American elm, oak, ponderosa pine, walnut, and peachleaf willow. Isolated stands of trees occur throughout the state in places where people have planted trees to act as windbreaks and to control erosion.

**Wild Plants:** Some two hundred species of grasses grow in Nebraska—more varieties than in any other state. The uncultivated regions of eastern Nebraska are covered with such tall grasses as blue stem. Buffalo and other short grasses are found in the west. Other plants commonly found in the state include phloxes, violets, blue flags, larkspurs, spiderworts, columbines, poppies, wild roses, goldenrod, sunflowers, and such shrubs as wild plum and chokecherry.

**Animals:** Antelope and elk are found in small numbers in the northwest corner of the state. Other animals found in the state include deer, badgers, coyotes, foxes, muskrats, opossums, prairie dogs, jackrabbits, raccoons, skunks, and squirrels. Buffalo, once found throughout Nebraska, today exist only in captive herds.

Small numbers of elk can be found in northwestern Nebraska.

**Birds:** Game birds such as ducks, geese, pheasants, and quail are plentiful. Wild turkeys, though less plentiful, are found throughout the state. Each spring, the world's largest concentration of sandhill cranes congregates in the Platte River Valley west of Grand Island.

**Fish:** Freshwater fish found in the state's rivers and lakes include bass, bluegill, carp, catfish, crappie, perch, pike, trout, and walleye.

## GOVERNMENT

Like the federal government, the Nebraska state government is divided into three branches—executive, judicial, and legislative.

The executive branch, headed by the governor, is responsible for administering the laws of the state. The governor, lieutenant governor, attorney general, secretary of state, treasurer, and auditor are elected to four-year terms. The governor and treasurer may serve no more than two consecutive terms. When the state legislature passes a bill, it is forwarded to the governor. If the governor signs the bill or does nothing about it for five days, the bill becomes law. The governor may veto (refuse to sign) a bill. However, if three-fifths of the senators vote to override the governor's veto, the bill becomes law.

The state's one-house nonpartisan legislature is the only one of its kind among the states. This unicameral legislature is currently made up of forty-nine senators, one from each of the state's forty-nine legislative districts. The districts have been drawn so that each contains approximately 30,000 constituents. If the population changes, the number of districts in the state may change. State senators are elected without reference to political party labels. The senators are expected to serve the interests of their constituents rather than the platform of a political party. Senators are elected to four-year terms, but elections are staggered so that only half of the legislature is up for election every two years. This is to insure that no more than half of the legislature will be overturned in a single election. Unless a special session is called by the governor, the entire legislature meets once a year for sixty days (in even-numbered years) or ninety days (in odd-numbered years). A legislative council meets between sessions.

The judicial branch interprets the law and tries cases. The highest court in the state is the seven-member supreme court, composed of a chief justice and six associate justices. Below the supreme court is a system of twenty-one district courts presided over by a total of forty-seven district-court judges. Initially, a judge is appointed by the governor, who follows the recommendations of a nominating committee. After serving three years, each judge must run for election. If a judge is retained, he or she must run for reelection every six years. Each of the state's ninety-three counties has a court presided over by a county judge who is elected to a four-year term. Omaha and Lincoln maintain municipal and juvenile court districts.

**Number of Counties:** 93

**U.S. Representatives:** 3

**Electoral Votes:** 5

**Voting Qualifications:** United States citizen, eighteen years of age, six months residency in the state, forty days residency in the county, and ten days residency in the election district

## EDUCATION

Nebraska's first school was established in 1820. The state's first free-school law was passed in 1855, and the first compulsory school-attendance law was passed in 1891. Today, all Nebraska children between the ages of seven and fifteen are required to attend school. Approximately 267,000 students attend Nebraska public elementary and secondary schools. Every year, Nebraska spends about $3,500 per student. About 48,000 students attend private elementary and secondary schools.

Nebraska, like many other states, has a growing number of publicly controlled community, junior, and technical colleges. Central Community College has campuses in Grand Island, Hastings, and Columbus. Southeast Community College has campuses in Beatrice, Fairbury, Lincoln, and Milford. Other community colleges include Metropolitan Technical Community College in Omaha, McCook Community College in McCook, Mid-Plains Community College in North Platte,

**A herd of cattle grazing on the plains of southern Nebraska**

and Northeast Community College in Norfolk. York College in York is privately endowed.

A total of sixteen degree-granting colleges in Nebraska are accredited by the North Central Association of Colleges and Schools. The University of Nebraska, established in 1869, is by far the largest. The university's Lincoln campus serves nearly twenty-five thousand students. About fourteen thousand students attend the university's Omaha campus, and twenty-five hundred students attend the University of Nebraska Medical Center, also in Omaha. Other major universities and colleges in Nebraska are Bishop Clarkson College of Nursing, College of St. Mary, and Creighton University, all in Omaha; Nebraska Wesleyan University and Union College, both in Lincoln; Bellevue College; Hastings College; Kearney State College; Peru State College; Wayne State College; Midland Lutheran College, in Fremont; and Concordia Teachers College, in Seward.

## ECONOMY AND INDUSTRY

### Principal Products:

*Agriculture:* Beef cattle, corn, hogs, soybeans, wheat, dairy products, poultry and eggs, sheep, hay, potatoes, sorghum grain, sugar beets, apples

*Manufacturing:* Processed foods, meat packing, nonelectrical machinery, electrical machinery, metals, printing and publishing, transportation equipment, construction material, chemicals

*Natural Resources:* Fertile soil, oil, natural gas, sand, gravel, clay, limestone

Railroad tracks near Grand Island

**Business and Trade:** Insurance, finance, and real-estate industries form the largest block of business activity in the state. These industries account for $4.04 billion annually—about 16 percent of the state's total economic performance. Omaha is the headquarters of Mutual of Omaha, the largest private health-insurance corporation in the world. Wholesale and retail trade also provide about 16 percent of the state's gross product, and employ nearly 157,000 people.

**Communication:** The state's first newspaper, the *Nebraska Palladium and Platte Valley Advocate,* was established in Bellevue in 1854. Of the state's 20 daily newspapers, the *Omaha World-Herald,* the *Lincoln Journal,* and the *Lincoln Star* have the largest circulations. There are about 165 other newspapers, most of them weeklies. The University of Nebraska Press is an important book publisher in the state. Approximately 60 magazines are published in Nebraska. The state's first radio station, WCAJ, operated by Nebraska Wesleyan University, began broadcasting from Lincoln in 1921. WOAW (now WOW), Nebraska's first commercial radio station, began broadcasting from Omaha in 1923. Two Omaha television stations began broadcasting in 1949; WOW-TV and KMTV. Today, approximately 15 television stations and 115 radio stations operate within the state.

**Transportation:** Located near the center of the continental United States, Nebraska is within a one-day drive of such major cities as Chicago, St. Louis, Kansas City, Minneapolis, Denver, and Salt Lake City. For overland carriers, this represents a major heartland market of some 50 million customers. Nebraska's

**A church at the Stuhr Museum of the Prairie Pioneer**

main highway, Interstate 80, is an east-west route across the state. Nebraska has a total of 82,500 mi. (132,771 km) of paved roads.

Of the state's many rivers, only the Missouri is useful for shipping. Omaha is the principal Missouri River port in Nebraska. Other ports on the Missouri include Blair, Bellevue, Plattsmouth, Nebraska City, and South Sioux City.

Freight service is offered by five railroad lines in Nebraska, and five cities are served by passenger trains. Approximately 5,000 mi. (8,047 km) of track are currently in service. The huge Bailey Railroad Yard, operated near North Platte by the Union Pacific, is the nation's largest railroad classification yard. Nebraska has about 110 public airports and 210 private airports. A total of 16 commercial airlines serve the state.

## SOCIAL AND CULTURAL LIFE

**Museums:** One of the nation's most famous collections of Western American art is housed at the Joslyn Art Museum in Omaha. Displays range from ancient American Indian artifacts to contemporary art. Two museums on the University of Nebraska campus at Lincoln—the Sheldon Memorial Art Gallery and the Christlieb Western Art Collection—have sizable art collections. A third museum operated by the university is Morrill Hall in Lincoln, nicknamed "Elephant Hall" because of its huge collection of mammoth fossils. Also in Lincoln is the Nebraska State Historical Society Museum, the largest of five museums operated by the state's historical society. Other significant museums scattered around the state include the Strategic Air Command Museum near Bellevue, the Stuhr Museum of the Prairie

Pioneer in Grand Island, and the Willa Cather Historical Center in Red Cloud. The Great Plains Black History Museum claims to have the most complete exhibit of black American history west of the Mississippi. One of Nebraska's most unusual museums is Harold Warp's Pioneer Village near Minden, an indoor/outdoor museum that features a huge collection of artifacts spanning from the 1830s to the present.

**Libraries:** The first library in Nebraska was established at Fort Atkinson in 1820. The Kansas-Nebraska Act established a territorial library in 1854; it is now the state law library. Nebraska's first public library was founded in Omaha in 1871. Nebraska has 550 school libraries, 270 public libraries, 35 college and university libraries, and 70 specialty libraries. The state's largest library, with more than 2 million volumes, is the University of Nebraska library in Lincoln. The university also maintains a large library on its Omaha campus. Other major libraries include the City Library and the Nebraska State Historical Society Library, both in Lincoln; the Omaha Public Library; and the Creighton University Library, also in Omaha.

**Performing Arts:** The state's mecca for performing arts is the Orpheum Theater in Omaha, home of the Omaha Symphony Orchestra, the Omaha Opera, and the Omaha Ballet. Many touring companies, including road shows of Broadway plays, also perform at the Orpheum. Productions are also staged at the Omaha Community Playhouse. Nebraska Wesleyan University maintains the oldest theatrical repertory company in the state. The company performs various plays at the Village Theater in Brownville. Other theatrical performances, including those associated with the University of Nebraska, are staged in Lincoln and Omaha.

**Sports and Recreation:** Every spring, Omaha's Rosenblatt Stadium hosts the annual National Collegiate Athletic Association College World Series baseball games. In the fall, Nebraskans avidly follow the exploits of the University of Nebraska Cornhuskers football team, a perennial Big Eight champion. The Cornhuskers' home games are played at the University of Nebraska's Memorial Stadium in Lincoln. A number of major rodeos, and dozens of smaller ones, are featured throughout the state at various times. The World Championship Rodeo is held in the fall at Omaha's Ak-Sar-Ben Field and Coliseum. The Buffalo Bill Rodeo is staged during Nebraskaland Days in June at the Buffalo Bill Ranch State Historical Park near North Platte. North Platte Nite Rodeos are performed at the same location.

The Henry Doorly Zoo in Omaha houses animals in outdoor enclosures resembling natural habitats. The Folsom Children's Zoo in Lincoln features a train ride and many "pettable" animals. The unique Ak-Sar-Ben Aquarium near Gretna includes an old-time fish hatchery on the grounds. Peony Park in Omaha features a number of thrill rides.

More than two thousand lakes and thousands of miles of rivers and streams afford ample opportunities for fishing. Outdoor activities can be enjoyed at the state's six state parks and sixty-six state recreation areas. Indian Cave State Park near Shubert in the southwest corner of the state features preserved Indian writings on cave walls and three mi. (five km) of magnificent Missouri River bluffs. Spectacular scenery also prevails in the northeastern part of the state at Ponca and

**A Siberian Tiger relaxes in his outdoor habitat at the Henry Doorly Zoo in Omaha.**

Niobrara state parks. In the western part of Nebraska, Scotts Bluff National Monument, Chimney Rock National Historic Site, and Courthouse Rock and Jail Rock are popular tourist attractions.

### Historic Sites and Landmarks:

*Arbor Lodge State Historical Park and Tree Trail* in Nebraska City contains the restored mansion and orchards of J. Sterling Morton, the founder of Arbor Day.

*Buffalo Bill Ranch State Historical Park* near North Platte features the home of Wild West showman Buffalo Bill Cody, whose famous Wild West Show started in North Platte. Nightly rodeos are staged during the summer.

*Ferguson House* in Lincoln is the rehabilitated 1910 mansion of Nebraska businessman William Henry Ferguson. It is now used as a museum.

*Fontenelle Bank* in Bellevue is one of a number of historic buildings in Nebraska's oldest city. Used as a bank from 1856 to 1857, it has been preserved as one of Nebraska's oldest public buildings.

*Fort Atkinson State Historical Park*, north of Omaha, is a partially completed reconstruction of the first great military outpost west of the Missouri River. The fort was active from 1819 to 1827.

*Fort Hartsuff State Historical Park*, near Elyria, is a restoration of a fort that was built in 1874 to protect the Pawnee Indians from the Sioux.

**The restored Neligh Mills**

*Fort Kearny State Historical Park,* near Kearney, features re-creations of the stockade, blacksmith shop, and other structures of this historic fort on the Platte River.

*Fort Robinson State Park and Museum* in Crawford features a large and scenic recreational area and a historic fort, now used as a museum, that contains a number of buildings constructed in the late 1800s and early 1900s.

*General Crook House* in Omaha was once the headquarters of noted Indian fighter General George Crook. It is now a museum operated by the Douglas County Historical Society.

*Homestead National Monument,* near Beatrice, honors one of the earliest homestead claims in the state, made by Daniel Freeman in 1863. A variety of living-history displays depict pioneer soap making, candle making, cooking, farming, and schooling.

*Mormon Pioneer Cemetery* in Omaha contains the graves of nearly six hundred Mormon pioneers who died during the bitter winter of 1846-47.

*Neligh Mills* in Neligh is a restored flour mill operated by the Nebraska State Historical Society.

*Norris Home* in McCook was once the home of United States senator George Norris, the chief advocate of the unicameral state legislature. The house is now operated as a museum by the Nebraska State Historical Society.

*Pike-Pawnee National Landmark,* near Guide Rock, marks the site of a large Pawnee village that was visited by Zebulon Pike in 1806.

**Fort Kearny State Historical Park**

*Pony Express Station* in Gothenburg is a restoration of one of the stops at which Pony Express riders changed horses while advancing the mails in Nebraska in the early 1860s. It has been moved from its original site and is now surrounded by a municipal park.

*Rock Creek Station,* near Fairbury, is a restoration of a Pony Express station.

*Roubidoux Pass,* near Bridgeport, was traveled by thousands of covered wagons between 1843 and 1851. Pioneer graves are still visible along the road.

*William Jennings Bryan Home* in Lincoln is the former residence of the famous orator and three-time presidential candidate.

**Other Interesting Places to Visit:**

*Agate Fossil Beds National Monument,* near Harrison, is one of the richest sources of prehistoric fossils in the United States.

*Ak-Sar-Ben Aquarium* in Gretna is a popular place to view native and exotic water life.

*Belle of Bellevue,* on the Missouri River near Bellevue, is a large excursion boat that offers family cruises.

**A waterfall at Fort Niobrara National Wildlife Refuge**

*Boys Town*, near Omaha, was established in 1917 by Father Edward Flanagan as a home and school for neglected and troubled boys. Today, the home welcomes both boys and girls.

*Chimney Rock National Historic Site*, near Bayard, features an unusual rock formation that rises like a great stone chimney 500 ft. (152 m) above the North Platte River.

*DeSoto National Wildlife Refuge*, near Blair, is noted for the large numbers of visiting waterfowl that can be seen in March and October.

*Fort Niobrara National Wildlife Refuge*, north of Valentine, maintains sizable herds of elk, buffalo, antelope, and Texas longhorn cattle.

*Governor's Mansion* in Lincoln is the home of Nebraska's current governor.

*Mueller Planetarium* in Lincoln features images of the night sky projected onto a domed ceiling.

*Old Market* in Omaha is a Victorian-style shopping and restaurant area that sometimes features entertainment and craft fairs.

*Snake River Falls*, near Valentine, is the largest waterfall in Nebraska. It is surrounded by a lovely wooded canyon.

**Toadstool Park in the Oglala National Grasslands features unusual rock formations.**

*Starke Barn* in Red Cloud is the largest circular-frame barn in the United States. Built in 1902, the three-story structure is held together without the use of nails, spikes, or pegs.

*State Capitol* in Lincoln was designed by Bertram Grosvenor Goodhue and was built between 1922 and 1932.

*Strategic Air Command Museum* in Bellevue features displays and shows about the Strategic Air Command (SAC).

*Toadstool Park,* in the Oglala National Grasslands north of Crawford, features unusually shaped rock formations.

*Valentine National Wildlife Area,* south of Valentine, attracts a wide variety of waterfowl and other wildlife to its shallow lakes.

## IMPORTANT DATES

c. 10,000 B.C. — Paleo-Indians roam the Nebraska plains

c. 500 B.C.-A.D. 1 — People of the Archaic Culture inhabit the area now known as Nebraska

c. 100-900 — During what is known as the Woodland Period, Indians living on the Nebraska plains form settlements and engage in such activities as agriculture and pottery making

1541—Francisco Vásquez de Coronado and a Spanish army reach present-day Kansas and claim vast amounts of territory for Spain, including the land of present-day Nebraska

1682—René-Robert Cavelier, Sieur de La Salle, claims all the land drained by the Mississippi River, including Nebraska, for France

1714—Étienne Veniard de Bourgmont travels up the Missouri River and reaches the mouth of the Platte River

1720—Spanish forces under Pedro de Villasur withdraw after being badly defeated by Pawnee Indians near present-day Columbus

1739-40—French explorers Pierre and Paul Mallet cross Nebraska, probably becoming the first white men to cross the region

1763—By the Treaty of Paris ending the French and Indian War, France cedes the Louisiana territory, including the land of present-day Nebraska, to Spain

1800—Spain cedes Louisiana back to France

1803—The land of present-day Nebraska becomes American territory when the United States buys Louisiana from France

1804—Meriwether Lewis and William Clark explore eastern Nebraska

1806—Lieutenant Zebulon Pike travels through south-central Nebraska

1807-20—Spanish American trader Manuel Lisa establishes a number of fur-trading posts along the Missouri River

c. 1809—Ramsay Crooks and Robert McClellan build a trading post near present-day Omaha

1813—On his return to the East from Oregon, Robert Stuart leads a party through Nebraska on a path along the North Platte and Platte rivers that becomes known as the Oregon Trail

1819—Soldiers under the command of General Henry Atkinson build Fort Atkinson on the west bank of the Missouri River just north of present-day Omaha

1823—Andrew Drips builds a trading post at Bellevue that is generally regarded as the first permanent white settlement in Nebraska

1824—William Ashley leads a group of fur trappers along the Platte Valley on their way to the Rocky Mountains

1835 — The first group of Christian missionaries bound for Oregon passes through Nebraska and the Platte Valley along the Oregon Trail

1841 — The first wagon train of settlers bound for Oregon passes through the Platte Valley along the Oregon Trail

1843 — The enormous westward movement along the Oregon Trail that becomes known as the "Great Migration" begins

1848 — Fort Kearny is established near the present town of Kearney to protect the thousands of settlers following the Oregon Trail

1854 — Congress passes the Kansas-Nebraska Act, creating the territories of Nebraska and Kansas

1862 — Congress passes the Homestead Act

1863 — One of the first homesteads in Nebraska Territory is claimed by Daniel Freeman in present-day Gage County

1867 — Nebraska is admitted to the Union as the thirty-seventh state; after bitter feuding, Lincoln is selected as the state capital; the stretch of the Union Pacific Railroad crossing Nebraska is completed

1872 — Arbor Day becomes a state holiday

1874-77 — Many Nebraska crops are destroyed by repeated grasshopper attacks

1875 — Present state constitution is adopted

1877 — Oglala Sioux chief Crazy Horse surrenders at Fort Robinson

1890 — Nebraska suffers a terrible drought; due to the drought, land prices collapse, farm prices drop, and credit becomes overextended

1896 — William Jennings Bryan of Nebraska becomes the Democratic (and People's party) nominee for president of the United States

1902 — Congress passes the Reclamation Act, setting the stage for a vast irrigation project on the North Platte River

1904 — The Kinkaid Act encourages settlement of the Sand Hills region

1917 — Boys Town is established in Omaha by Father Edward Flanagan

1932 — Present state capitol is completed

1934 — The state constitution is amended to create a unicameral legislature

1937—First session of the state's unicameral legislature is held

1939—Oil is discovered near Falls City in southeastern Nebraska

1942—Kingsley Dam, creating Lake McConaughy on the North Platte River, is completed

1944—Congress authorizes the Missouri River Basin Project

1954—Nebraska celebrates its territorial centennial

1956—Gavins Point Dam is completed, creating Lewis and Clark Lake along the Missouri River

1967—Nebraska celebrates its state centennial; a state sales tax and income tax are created

1974—Gerald R. Ford, born in Omaha, becomes the thirty-eighth president of the United States

1986—Nebraska becomes the first state to have a gubernatorial race in which the candidates of both major political parties are women

1987—Kay Orr is elected governor of Nebraska, becoming the first woman Republican governor in United States history

## IMPORTANT PEOPLE

**Grace Abbott** (1878-1939), born in Grand Island; social reformer; in 1908 founded the Immigrants' Protective League in Chicago; head of the Immigrants' Protective League (1908-17); chief of the United States Children's Bureau (1921-34)

**Bess Streeter Aldrich** (1881-1954), novelist and short-story writer; moved to Nebraska with her husband in 1909; wrote a number of stories and novels set in Nebraska, including *The Rim of the Prairie* and *A Lantern in Her Hand*

**Fred Astaire** (1899-1987), born Frederick Austerlitz in Omaha; dancer and actor; known for his graceful dancing and his air of sophistication; appeared in more than thirty-five films including *Top Hat, Holiday Inn, Daddy Long Legs,* and *Silk Stockings*

**Maximilian Adelbert (Max) Baer** (1909-1959), born in Omaha; boxer, actor; world heavyweight champion (1934-35); starred in the film *The Prize Fighter and the Lady*

**FRED ASTAIRE**

**George Wells Beadle** (1903-    ), born in Wahoo; scientist and educator; shared the 1958 Nobel Prize in physiology; president of the University of Chicago (1961-68)

**Marlon Brando** (1924-    ), born in Omaha; actor; starred in such films as *A Streetcar Named Desire, Mutiny on the Bounty,* and *The Wild One*; won the Academy Award for best actor for his roles in *On the Waterfront* (1954) and *The Godfather* (1972)

**MARLON BRANDO**

**William Jennings Bryan** (1860-1925), lawyer, politician, orator; known as the "Commoner," he was the greatest orator of his time; moved to Lincoln in 1887; U.S. representative (1891-95); editor of the *Omaha World-Herald* (1894-96); his Populist sentiments excited Nebraska farmers; advocated the free coinage of silver; made three unsuccessful bids for the presidency of the United States (1896, 1900, 1908); secretary of state under President Woodrow Wilson (1913-15); assisted the prosecution in the famous Scopes trial

**Johnny Carson** (1925-    ), entertainer; grew up in Norfolk; host of the long-running television show "The Tonight Show"

**Willa Sibert Cather** (1873-1947), writer; moved to Nebraska from Virginia at the age of ten; wrote such novels about pioneer life in Nebraska as *O Pioneers!* and *My Antonia*; received the 1923 Pulitzer Prize in fiction for *One of Ours*, also set in Nebraska

**WILLIAM JENNINGS BRYAN**

**Richard (Dick) Cavett** (1936-    ), born in Gibbon; interviewer and author; host of a number of network and syndicated television talk shows

**William Frederick "Buffalo Bill" Cody** (1846-1917), frontiersman, scout, showman; served as a scout for the military (1863, 1868-72, 1876); became an actor in 1872, when he began starring in *Scouts of the Prairies*; in 1878 built a ranch near North Platte; in 1882, staged the "Old Glory Blowout" in North Platte, considered the "granddaddy of all American rodeos"; in 1883 organized Buffalo Bill's Wild West Show; toured the United States and Europe with the show (1883-1916); he and the show wintered every year at his North Platte ranch

**JOHNNY CARSON**

**Edward Creighton** (1820-1874), businessman; helped build the telegraph line from Omaha to Sacramento, thereby opening up the American West to communication; Creighton University was founded and endowed in his name

**Michael Cudahy** (1841-1910), meat packer; introduced refrigeration at meat-packing plants; founder and president of Cudahy Packing Company in Omaha

**Sandy Dennis** (1937-    ), born in Hastings; actress; won the 1966 Academy Award for best supporting actress for her role in *Who's Afraid of Virginia Woolf*

**WILLA CATHER**

**EDWARD FLANAGAN**

**HENRY FONDA**

**GERALD FORD**

**HAROLD LLOYD**

**Edward Joseph Flanagan** (1886-1948), clergyman and social activist; ordained Roman Catholic priest (1912); founded the Workingmen's Hotel for destitute men in Omaha (1914); founded Father Flanagan's Home for Boys in Omaha (1917), a home and school for neglected and troubled boys; in 1918, moved the facility west of Omaha, where it became an incorporated village known as Boys Town

**Henry Jaynes Fonda** (1905-1982), born in Grand Island; actor; known for his midwestern persona and his portrayals of strong, decent, straightforward men; appeared in more than eighty films, including *Young Mr. Lincoln, The Grapes of Wrath*, and *Mister Roberts*; won the 1981 Academy Award for best actor for his role in *On Golden Pond*

**Gerald Rudolph Ford** (1913-    ), born in Omaha; thirty-eighth president of the United States (1974-77); U.S. Naval officer in World War II (1942-46); U.S. representative from Michigan (1948-73); House Minority Leader (1965-73); served as vice-president of the United States after the resignation of Spiro Agnew (1973-74); succeeded to the presidency after President Nixon resigned as a result of the Watergate scandal

**Robert (Bob) Gibson** (1935-    ), born in Omaha; professional baseball player; pitcher for the St. Louis Cardinals (1959-75); named Most Valuable Player in the National League (1968); received the National League Cy Young Award (1986, 1970); admitted to the Baseball Hall of Fame (1981)

**Joyce Clyde Hall** (1891-1978), born in David City; businessman; founder of Hallmark Cards

**Francis La Flesche** (1857-1932), born near Bellevue; ethnologist; son of an Omaha chief; worked for the Bureau of American Ethnology (1910-29); champion of Indian rights; wrote a memoir, *The Middle Five*, and a number of books about American Indians, including *A Dictionary of the Osage Language* and (with Alice Fletcher) *The Omaha Tribe*

**Susette La Flesche** (1854-1903), born near Bellevue; sister of Francis La Flesche; social reformer, writer; daughter of an Omaha chief; known publicly as "Bright Eyes," the English translation of *Inshta Theumba*, her Indian name; champion of Indian rights; traveled east to speak out against forced removal of the Omaha and Ponca Indians (1879); helped bring about passage of the Dawes Severalty Act, which gave individual Indians, under certain conditions, the right to own land; wrote stories of Indian life

**Harold Clayton Lloyd** (1893-1971), born in Burchard; comic actor, writer, producer; known for his portrayal of a shy, bespectacled character who wore a straw hat and who often narrowly escaped from dangerous situations; appeared in more than three hundred silent films, including *Safety Last, The Freshman*, and *The Milky Way*

**Malcolm X** (1925-1965), born Malcolm Little in Omaha; religious leader, political activist, author; brilliant orator who advocated racial pride and black separatism; founded the Organization of Afro-American Unity (1964); wrote *The Autobiography of Malcolm X* (1965); assassinated in Harlem

**Samuel Roy McKelvie** (1881-1956), politician, publisher; governor of Nebraska (1919-23); member of President Hoover's Federal Farm Board (1929-31); edited and published the *Nebraska Farmer* (1905-56)

**Julius Sterling Morton** (1832-1902), politician, conservationist; settled in Nebraska in 1854; secretary of Nebraska Territory (1858-61); founded the *Nebraska City News*; founder of Arbor Day (1872); U.S. secretary of agriculture (1893-97)

**John Gneisenau Neihardt** (1881-1973), poet and author; known for his interest in the Indians of the Great Plains; moved to Wayne, Nebraska, in 1891; lived with the Omaha Indians of Nebraska (1901-07); named Poet Laureate of Nebraska (1921); best-known work was *Black Elk Speaks*, a biography of a Sioux medicine man

**George William Norris** (1861-1944), politician; known for his independent thinking and his refusal to be influenced by party politics; moved to Nebraska in 1885; U.S. representative (1903-13); U.S. senator (1913-43); opposed American entry into World War I; led the fight to overthrow the dictatorial rule of Speaker of the House Joseph Cannon (1910); sponsored the legislation that led to creation of the Tennessee Valley Authority (1933); helped secure passage of the 20th (Lame Duck) Amendment to the U.S. Constitution (1932); influential supporter of the Nebraska constitutional amendment creating a unicameral state legislature

**Louise Pound** (1872-1958), born in Lincoln; educator and author; taught English at the University of Nebraska (1897-45); folklorist and expert on the English ballad; edited the journal *American Speech* (1925-33)

**Roscoe Pound** (1870-1964), born in Lincoln; brother of Louise Pound; scholar and educator; taught law at the University of Nebraska (1890-1903), Northwestern University (1907-09), the University of Chicago (1909-10), and Harvard University (1910-37); dean of Harvard Law School (1916-36); wrote extensively on the philosophy and practice of law

**Mari Sandoz** (1901-1966), born in Sheridan County; novelist and historian; author of many fictional and nonfictional accounts of pioneer life on the Great Plains, including *Old Jules, Crazy Horse,* and *Cheyenne Autumn*

**Anna Louise Strong** (1885-1970), born in Friend; journalist, child welfare worker; author of *Songs of the City, Children of the Revolution,* and *One Fifth of Mankind*

MALCOLM X

JOHN NEIHARDT

GEORGE NORRIS

MARI SANDOZ

131

**DARRYL ZANUCK**

**Robert Taylor** (1911-1969), born Spangle Brugh in Filley; actor; appeared in such films as *Quo Vadis* and *The Magnificent Obsession*

**Darryl Francis Zanuck** (1902-1979), born in Wahoo; film producer; leading force behind the film production company 20th Century Fox; produced such famous films as *The Grapes of Wrath, How Green Was My Valley, Gentlemen's Agreement, The Sound of Music,* and *Patton*

## GOVERNORS

| | | | |
|---|---|---|---|
| David Butler | 1867-1871 | Charles W. Bryan | 1923-1925 |
| W.H. James | 1871-1873 | Adam McMullen | 1925-1929 |
| Robert W. Furnas | 1873-1875 | Arthur J. Weaver | 1929-1931 |
| Silas Garber | 1875-1879 | Charles W. Bryan | 1931-1935 |
| Albinus Nance | 1879-1883 | Robert Leroy Cochran | 1935-1941 |
| James W. Dawes | 1883-1887 | Dwight Griswold | 1941-1947 |
| John M. Thayer | 1887-1892 | Val Peterson | 1947-1953 |
| James E. Boyd | 1892-1893 | Robert B. Crosby | 1953-1955 |
| Lorenzo Crounse | 1893-1895 | Victor E. Anderson | 1955-1959 |
| Silas A. Holcomb | 1895-1899 | Ralph G. Brooks | 1959-1960 |
| William A. Poynter | 1899-1901 | Dwight W. Burney | 1960-1961 |
| Charles H. Dietrich | 1901 | Frank B. Morrison | 1961-1967 |
| Ezra P. Savage | 1901-1903 | Norbert T. Tiemann | 1967-1971 |
| John H. Mickey | 1903-1907 | J. James Exon | 1971-1979 |
| George L. Sheldon | 1907-1909 | Charles Thone | 1979-1983 |
| Ashton C. Shallenberger | 1909-1911 | Robert Kerrey | 1983-1987 |
| Chester H. Aldrich | 1911-1913 | Kay A. Orr | 1987- |
| John H. Morehead | 1913-1917 | | |
| Keith Neville | 1917-1919 | | |
| Samuel R. McKelvie | 1919-1923 | | |

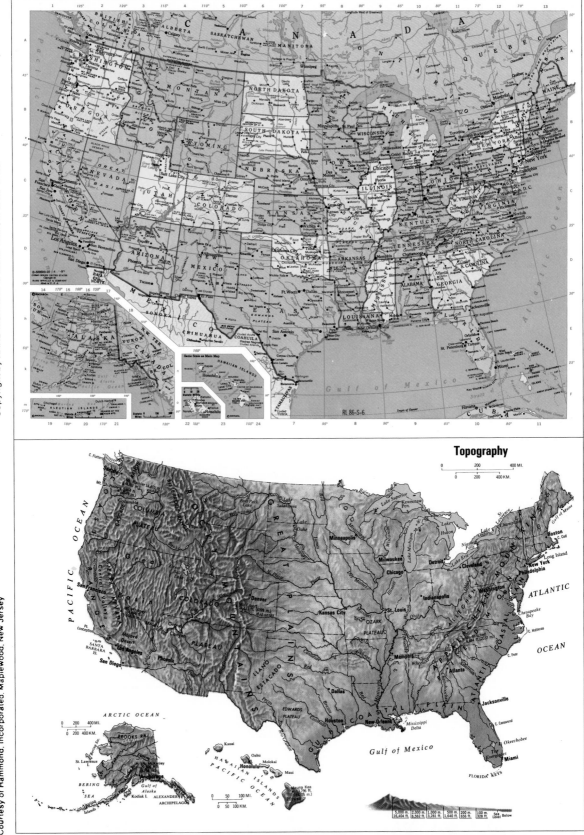

## Topography

## MAP KEY

|  |  |
|---|---|
| Agate Fossil Beds National Monument | B1,2 |
| Ainsworth | B6 |
| Alda | C7,D7 |
| Alliance | B3 |
| Alma | D6 |
| Atlanta | D6 |
| Ansley | C6 |
| Arapahoe | D6 |
| Arlington | C9,g12 |
| Arnold | C5 |
| Ashland | C9,g12 |
| Atkinson | B7 |
| Auburn | D10 |
| Aurora | D7 |
| Axtell | D6 |
| Bancroft | B9 |
| Bartley | D5 |
| Bassett | B6 |
| Bayard | C2 |
| Beatrice | D9,h11 |
| Beaver City | D6 |
| Beaver Crossing | C8 |
| Beaver Lake (lake) | C9 |
| Beemer | B9 |
| Bellevue | C9,g12 |
| Bellwood | C8 |
| Bennet | C9,g12 |
| Bennington | C9,g12 |
| Bertrand | D6 |
| Big Blue (river) | C,D8,9 |
| Big Nemaha (river) | D9,10 |
| Big Springs | C4 |
| Birdwood Creek (creek) | C4,5 |
| Blair | C9,g12 |
| Bloomfield | B8 |
| Blue Creek (creek) | C4 |
| Blue Hill | D7 |
| Blue Springs | D9 |
| Box Butte Creek (creek) | B,C3 |
| Boys Town | C9,g12 |
| Bridgeport | C2 |
| Broken Bow | C6 |
| Brownville | D10 |
| Burwell | C6 |
| Butte | B7 |
| Cairo | D7 |
| Calamus River (river) | B,C5,6 |
| Callaway | C5 |
| Cambridge | D5 |
| Carter Lake | g12 |
| Cedar (river) | B,C7 |
| Cedar Bluffs | C9,g11 |
| Central City | C,D7 |
| Ceresco | C9,g12 |
| Chadron | B3 |
| Chappell | C3 |
| Chimney Rock (rock) | C2 |
| Clarkson | C8 |
| Clay Center | D7 |
| Coleridge | B8 |
| Columbus | C8 |
| Cortland | D9 |
| Cozad | D6 |

|  |  |
|---|---|
| Crawford | B2 |
| Creighton | B8 |
| Crete | D9 |
| Crofton | B8 |
| Culbertson | D5 |
| Curtis | D5 |
| Dakota City | B9 |
| Dannebrog | C7 |
| David City | C8 |
| De Witt | D9 |
| Decatur | B9 |
| Deshler | D8 |
| Dodge | C9 |
| Doniphan | D7 |
| Dorchester | D8 |
| Driftwood Creek (creek) | D4,5 |
| Eagle | h12 |
| Edgar | D8 |
| Edison | D6 |
| Elgin | B8 |
| Elkhorn | C9,g12 |
| Elkhorn River (river) | B7,8,C8,9,g12 |
| Elm Creek | D6 |
| Elmwood | D9,h12 |
| Elwood | D6 |
| Emerson | B9 |
| Enders Reservoir (reservoir) | D4 |
| Ewing | B7 |
| Exeter | D8 |
| Fairbury | D8 |
| Fairfield | D7 |
| Falls City | D10 |
| Fairmont | D8 |
| Franklin | D7 |
| Fremont | C9,g11 |
| Frenchman Creek (creek) | D4 |
| Friend | D8 |
| Ft. Calhoun | C9,g12 |
| Fullerton | C8 |
| Geneva | D8 |
| Genoa | C8 |
| Gering | C2 |
| Gibbon | D7 |
| Gordon | B3 |
| Gothenburg | D5 |
| Grand Island | D7 |
| Grant | C4 |
| Greeley | C7 |
| Greenwood | C9,g12 |
| Gretna | C9,g12 |
| Guide Rock | D7 |
| Harlan County Lake (lake) | D6 |
| Harrison | B2 |
| Harry Strunk Lake (lake) | D5 |
| Hartington | B8 |
| Harvard | D7 |
| Hastings | D7 |
| Hat Creek (creek) | B3 |
| Hay Springs | B3 |
| Hebron | D8 |
| Hemingford | B2 |
| Henderson | D8 |
| Hershey | C4 |
| Hickman | C9,g12 |
| Highest Point in Nebraska | C1 |
| Hogback Mountain (mountain) | C2 |
| Holdrege | D7 |
| Holt Creek (creek) | B6,7 |
| Homer | B9 |
| Homestead National Monument | D9 |
| Hooper | C9,g12 |

|  |  |
|---|---|
| Howells | C8 |
| Hugh Butler Lake (reservoir) | D5 |
| Humboldt | D10 |
| Humphrey | C8 |
| Imperial | D4 |
| Indianola | D5 |
| Inman | B7 |
| Jackson | B9 |
| Jansen | D8 |
| Johnson | D9,10 |
| Juniata | D7 |
| Kearney | D6 |
| Kenesaw | D7 |
| Keya Paha River (river) | B6,7 |
| Kimball | C2 |
| Kingsley Dam (dam) | C4 |
| La Vista | g12 |
| Laurel | B8 |
| Leigh | C8 |
| Lewellen | C3 |
| Lewis and Clark Lake (reservoir) | B8 |
| Lexington | D6 |
| Lincoln | D9,h11 |
| Lindsay | C8 |
| Litchfield | D6,C3 |
| Little Blue (river) | C8 |
| Lodgepole | C3 |
| Lodgepole Creek (creek) | C1,2 |
| Logan Creek (creek) | B,C8,9 |
| Long Pine | B6 |
| Loomis | D6 |
| Louisville | C,D9,g12 |
| Loup River (river) | C7,8 |
| Loup City | C7 |
| Lyman | C1 |
| Lynch | B7 |
| Lyons | C9 |
| Madison | C8 |
| Madrid | D4 |
| Malcolm | C9 |
| Maloney Lake (lake) | D4,5 |
| Malmo | C9 |
| Manley | h12 |
| Marquette | D8 |
| Martinsburg | B9 |
| Mason City | C7 |
| Maxwell | C5 |
| Maywood | D5 |
| McConaughy Lake (lake) | C4 |
| McCook | D4 |
| McCool Junction (junction) | D8 |
| McGrew | C2 |
| Mead | C9,g12 |
| Meadow Grove | B8 |
| Medicine Creek (creek) | D5 |
| Melbeta | C2 |
| Merna | C6 |
| Merritt Reservoir (reservoir) | B5 |
| Middle Loup River (river) | B4,5,C6,7 |
| Milford | D8 |
| Miller | D6 |
| Milligan | D8 |
| Minden | D7 |
| Missouri River (river) | B7,8,9,C9,10,D10,g,h13 |
| Mitchell | C2 |
| Monroe | C8 |
| Morrill | C2 |
| Morse Bluff | C9 |
| Mud Creek (creek) | D7 |
| Mullen | B4 |
| Murdock | h12 |
| Murray | D10,h13 |
| North Bend | C9 |
| Naper | B6 |
| Nebraska City | D10,h13 |
| Nehawka | D10,h13 |
| Neligh | B7 |
| Nelson | D8 |
| Nemaha | D10 |
| Newcastle | B9 |
| Newman Grove | B8 |
| Newport | B6 |
| Nickerson | C9 |
| Niobrara | B7 |
| Niobrara River (river) | B2,3,4,5,6,7 |
| Norfolk | C8 |
| North Loup | C1,2,3,4,5 |
| North Loup (river) | C1,2,3,4,5 |
| North Platte River (river) | B4,C5,6,7 |
| North Platte | C4,5 |
| Northport | C8 |
| Oakdale | B8,9 |
| Oakland | B9 |
| Oconto | C6 |

|  |  |
|---|---|
| Octavia | C8 |
| Odell | D5 |
| Ogallala | D10 |
| Ohiowa | D8 |
| Omaha | C9,g12 |
| Omaha Indian Reservation | B9 |
| O'Neill | B7 |
| Ong | D8 |
| Orchard | B7 |
| Ord | C7 |
| Orleans | D6 |
| Osceola | C8 |
| Oshkosh | C3 |
| Osmond | B8 |
| Otoe | D9,h12 |
| Overton | D6 |
| Oxford | D6 |
| Page | B7 |
| Palisade | D4 |
| Palmer | C7 |
| Palmyra | D9,h12 |
| Panama | C9,g12 |
| Papillion | C9,g12 |
| Pawnee City | D9 |
| Paxton | D4 |
| Pender | B9 |
| Peru | D10 |
| Petersburg | B8 |
| Phillips | D7 |
| Pickrell | D9 |
| Pierce | B8 |
| Piger | C8 |
| Plainview | B8 |
| Platte River (river) | C5,D5,6,7,C7,8,9,10,g11,12,13 |
| Platte Center | C8 |
| Plattsmouth | C,D10,g,h13 |
| Pleasant Dale | D8 |
| Pleasanton | D6 |
| Plum Creek (creek) | B5,6 |
| Plum Creek (creek) | D8,9 |
| Plymouth | D8 |
| Polk | C8 |
| Ponca | B9 |
| Ponca Creek (creek) | B6 |
| Ponca Indian Reservation | B7 |
| Potter | C2 |
| Prague | C9 |
| Primrose | C7 |
| Prosser | D7 |
| Puckin (creek) | C2 |
| Ralston | C9,g12 |
| Randolph | B8 |
| Ravenna | D6 |
| Raymond | C9 |
| Red Cloud | D7 |
| Red Willow Creek (river) | D4,5 |
| Republican River (river) | B4,5,C6,7 |
| Republican City | D6 |
| Reynolds | D8 |
| Richland | C8 |
| Rising City | C8 |
| Riverdale | D6 |
| Riverton | D7 |
| Rock | h11 |
| Rockville | C7 |
| Rogers | C8 |
| Rosalie | B9 |
| Roseland | D7 |
| Royal | B7 |
| Rulo | D10 |
| Rush Creek (creek) | C2,3 |
| Rushville | B3 |
| Ruskin | D8 |
| St. Edward | C8 |
| St. Helena | B8 |
| St. Paul | C7 |
| Salem | D10 |
| Santee | B8 |
| Santee Indian Reservation | B8 |
| Sargent | C6 |
| Saronville | D7 |
| Schuyler | C8 |
| Scotia | C7 |
| Scotts Bluff National Monument | C2 |
| Scottsbluff | C2 |
| Scribner | C9 |
| Seneca | B5 |
| Seward | C8 |
| Shelby | C8 |
| Shelton | D7 |
| Sherman Reservoir (reservoir) | C7 |
| Shickley | D8 |
| Sholes | B8 |
| Shubert | D10 |
| Sidney | C3 |

|  |  |
|---|---|
| Silver Creek (creek) | g11,12 |
| Smithfield | D6 |
| Snake River (river) | B4 |
| Snake Falls (falls) | B5 |
| Snyder | C9 |
| South Bend | h12 |
| South Loup River (river) | C5,6,D6,7 |
| South Platte River (river) | C3,4,5 |
| South Sioux City | B9 |
| Spalding | C7 |
| Spencer | B7 |
| Sprague | C9,g12 |
| Springfield | B6 |
| Springview | B6 |
| Stamford | D6 |
| Stanton | C8 |
| Staplehurst | C8 |
| Stapleton | C5 |
| Steele City | D9 |
| Steinauer | D9 |
| Stella | D10 |
| Sterling | D8 |
| Stratton | D4 |
| Stromsburg | C8 |
| Stuart | B6 |
| Sumner | D7 |
| Superior | D6 |
| Surprise | C8 |
| Sutherland | C4 |
| Sutton | D8 |
| Swan Lake (lake) | C3 |
| Swanson Lake (lake) | D4 |
| Swanton | D8 |
| Syracuse | D9,h12 |
| Table Rock | D9 |
| Talmage | D8 |
| Tamora | C8 |
| Tarnov | C8 |
| Taylor | C6 |
| Tecumseh | D9 |
| Tekamah | C9 |
| Thayer | D8 |
| Thedford | C5 |
| Thurston | B9 |
| Tilden | B8 |
| Tobias | D8 |
| Trenton | D4 |
| Trumbull | D7 |
| Turkey Creek (creek) | D8,9 |
| Uehling | C9 |
| Ulysses | C8 |
| Unadilla | D8,9 |
| Union | D8 |
| Upland | D7 |
| Utica | D8 |
| Valentine | B5 |
| Valley | C9,g12 |
| Valparaiso | C8 |
| Venango | D3 |
| Verdigre | B7 |
| Verdel | B7 |
| Verdon | D10 |
| Virginia | D9 |
| Waco | D8 |
| Wahoo | C9,g11 |
| Wahoo Creek (creek) | g11,12 |
| Wakefield | B9 |
| Wallace | D4 |
| Walthill | B9 |
| Washington | g12 |
| Waterbury | B9 |
| Waterloo | g12 |
| Wauneta | D4 |
| Wausa | B8 |
| Wayne | B8 |
| Weeping Water | D9,h13 |
| West Point | C8 |
| Western | D8 |
| Weston | B8 |
| White River (river) | B2,3 |
| White Clay Creek (creek) | B3 |
| Wilcox | D6 |
| Wilsonville | D5 |
| Winnebago | B9 |
| Winnebago Indian Reservation | B9 |
| Winside | B8 |
| Winslow | C9 |
| Wisner | B8 |
| Wolbach | C7 |
| Wood River | D7 |
| Wymore | D9 |
| Wynot | B8 |
| York | D8 |
| Yutan | C9,g12 |

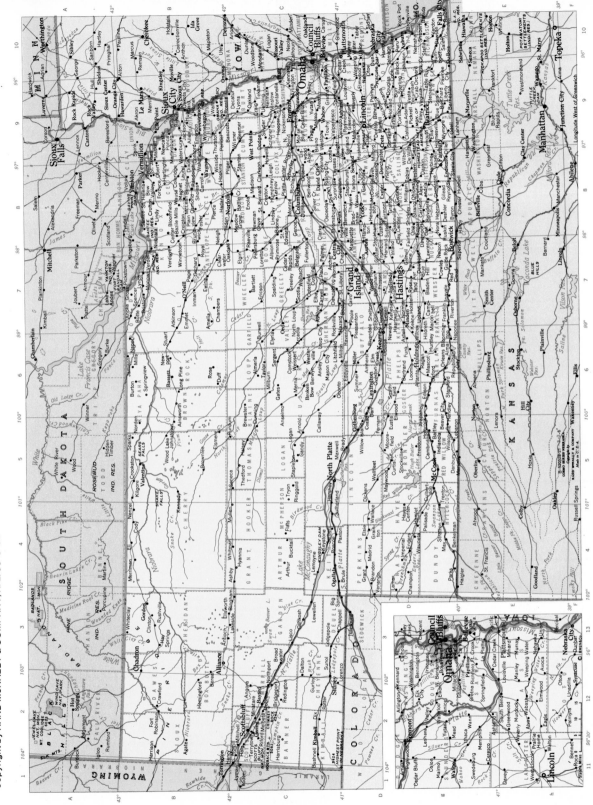

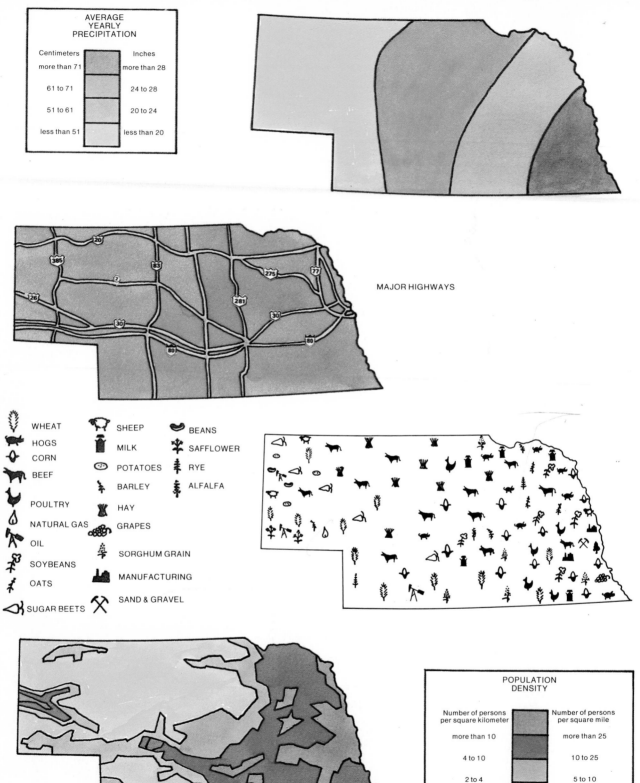

AVERAGE
YEARLY
PRECIPITATION

| Centimeters | | Inches |
|---|---|---|
| more than 71 | | more than 28 |
| 61 to 71 | | 24 to 28 |
| 51 to 61 | | 20 to 24 |
| less than 51 | | less than 20 |

MAJOR HIGHWAYS

WHEAT
HOGS
CORN
BEEF
POULTRY
NATURAL GAS
OIL
SOYBEANS
OATS
SUGAR BEETS

SHEEP
MILK
POTATOES
BARLEY
HAY
GRAPES
SORGHUM GRAIN
MANUFACTURING
SAND & GRAVEL

BEANS
SAFFLOWER
RYE
ALFALFA

POPULATION
DENSITY

| Number of persons per square kilometer | | Number of persons per square mile |
|---|---|---|
| more than 10 | | more than 25 |
| 4 to 10 | | 10 to 25 |
| 2 to 4 | | 5 to 10 |
| Less than 2 | | Less than 5 |

## TOPOGRAPHY

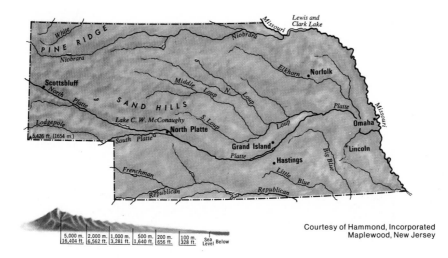

| 5,000 m. | 2,000 m. | 1,000 m. | 500 m. | 200 m. | 100 m. | Sea |
|----------|----------|----------|--------|--------|--------|-----|
| 16,404 ft. | 6,562 ft. | 3,281 ft. | 1,640 ft. | 656 ft. | 328 ft. | Level Below |

Topography map labels: PINE RIDGE, SAND HILLS, White, Niobrara, Missouri, Lewis and Clark Lake, Elkhorn, Norfolk, Scottsbluff, North Platte, Middle Loup, N. Loup, S. Loup, Loup, Platte, Omaha, Lodgepole, Lake C. W. McConaughy, North Platte, Grand Island, Lincoln, South Platte, Platte, Hastings, Big Blue, Little Blue, Frenchman, Republican, Republican, 5,426 ft. (1654 m.)

## COUNTIES

Counties map labels: Harrison, SIOUX, Chadron, DAWES, Rushville, SHERIDAN, BOX BUTTE, Alliance, Valentine, CHERRY, Ainsworth, BROWN, Bassett, ROCK, KEYA PAHA, Springview, HOLT, O'Neill, BOYD, Butte, KNOX, Center, Hartington, CEDAR, Poncaᵉ, DIXON, Dakota City, DAKOTA, SCOTTS BLUFF, Gering, MORRILL, Bridgeport, GARDEN, Oshkosh, Hyannis, GRANT, Mullen, HOOKER, Thedford, THOMAS, Brewster, BLAINE, LOUP, Taylor, GARFIELD, Burwell, WHEELER, Bartlett, BOONE, Albion, MADISON, Madison, Stanton, STANTON, CUMING, West Point, BURT, Tekamah, Neligh, ANTELOPE, PIERCE, Pierce, Wayne, WAYNE, THURSTON, Pender, Harrisburg, BANNER, Arthur, ARTHUR, MCPHERSON, Tryon, LOGAN, Stapleton, Broken Bow, CUSTER, Ord, VALLEY, GREELEY, Greeley, NANCE, Fullerton, PLATTE, Columbus, COLFAX, Schuyler, DODGE, Fremont, WASHINGTON, Blair, Kimball, KIMBALL, CHEYENNE, Sidney, DEUEL, Chappell, KEITH, Ogallala, North Platte, LINCOLN, Loup City, SHERMAN, HOWARD, St Paul, MERRICK, Central City, POLK, Osceola, David City, BUTLER, SAUNDERS, Wahoo, DOUGLAS, Omaha, Papillion, SARPY, PERKINS, Grant, DAWSON, Lexington, BUFFALO, Kearney, Grand Island, HALL, HAMILTON, Aurora, York, YORK, Seward, SEWARD, LINCOLN, LANCASTER, CASS, Plattsmouth, CHASE, Imperial, HAYES, Hayes Center, FRONTIER, Stockville, GOSPER, Elwood, PHELPS, Holdrege, KEARNEY, Minden, Hastings, ADAMS, CLAY, Clay Center, Geneva, FILLMORE, SALINE, Wilber, GAGE, Beatrice, JOHNSON, Tecumseh, NEMAHA, Auburn, Nebraska City, OTOE, DUNDY, Benkelman, HITCHCOCK, Trenton, McCook, RED WILLOW, FURNAS, Beaver City, HARLAN, Alma, FRANKLIN, Franklin, WEBSTER, Red Cloud, Nelson, NUCKOLLS, THAYER, Hebron, JEFFERSON, Fairbury, PAWNEE, Pawnee City, RICHARDSON, Falls City

A tallgrass prairie

# INDEX

**Page numbers that appear in boldface type indicate illustrations**

The stockyards in Omaha

**The stockyards in Omaha**

**Picture Identifications**

**Front cover:** The Omaha skyline behind the Central Park Mall Lagoon
**Back cover:** Courthouse Rock and Jail Rock
**Pages 2-3:** A windmill near Crawford
**Page 6:** The North Platte River at Scotts Bluff National Monument
**Pages 8-9:** Courthouse Rock and Jail Rock
**Page 20:** Montage of Nebraska residents
**Pages 26-27:** *Chimney Rock* by nineteenth-century artist Albert Bierstadt
**Page 36:** Detail from *Bellevue Agency, Post of Major Dougherty,* by nineteenth-century artist
Karl Bodmer
**Pages 48-49:** Detail from *The Emigrant Train Bedding Down for the Night,* an 1867 painting by
Benjamin Franklin Reinhart
**Pages 64-65:** Alfalfa being chopped at a farm in Valentine
**Pages 76-77:** The Ralston Purina plant in Lincoln
**Pages 88-89:** Canoeing on a Nebraska river
**Pages 96-97:** View of the Omaha skyline and the Heritage Statue
**Page 108:** Montage showing the state flag, the state tree (cottonwood), the state bird
(meadowlark), the state rock (prairie agate), and the state flower (goldenrod)

## Picture Acknowledgments

**Third Coast Stock Source:** © Robert E. Ridder: Front cover, Pages 47, 87, 92 (right)
© **James P. Rowan:** Pages 2-3, 123, 125, Back cover
© **H.W. Legg:** Pages 4, 118, 119
© **Jerry Hennen:** Pages 5, 18 (left), 108 (tree)
**H. Armstrong Roberts:** © M. Schneiders: Pages 6, 8-9, 13, 55, 105 (bottom left)
**Cameramann International, Ltd.:** Pages 11, 20 (middle right), 75, 76-77, 82, 83 (left), 84, 105 (top right), 110, 112, 117
**Root Resources:** © Vera Bradshaw: Page 12; © Mary M. Tremaine: Page 14; © Stan Strange: Pages 15 (right), 18 (right), 79, 92 (left), 102 (left); © Edgar Cheatham: Pages 20 (bottom left), 93, 100, 121; © L.E. Schaefer: Pages 51, 105 (bottom right); © James Blank: Pages 96-97; © Mary A. Root: Page 108 (flowers)
**Nawrocki Stock Photo:** © R.B. Pickering: Page 15 (left); © Les Van: Page 83 (inset)
**Camerique:** Pages 20 (top left), 72, 85 (both photos), 86, 115
**Tom Stack & Associates:** © Tom Stack: Pages 20 (top right), 25 (left); © John Shaw: Pages 25 (right), 138
**Nebraska Department of Economic Development:** © H.W. Legg: Pages 20 (bottom right), 22, 88-89, 94, 106
© **Chip & Rosa Maria Peterson:** Page 24
**The Bettmann Archive:** Pages 26-27, 43 (right), 57 (right), 61, 71, 128, 130 (Lloyd), 132
**Historical Pictures Service Inc., Chicago:** Pages 30, 33, 34, 52, 57 (left), 131 (Norris)
**The Granger Collection, New York:** Pages 31, 42, 43 (left), 45, 53, 60, 62, 68, 70, 105 (top left)
**North Wind:** Pages 32, 41 (both photos), 58
**Joslyn Art Museum, Omaha:** Page 36
**Nebraska State Historical Society:** Page 39
© **Reinhard Brucker:** Pages 44, 122, 124
**The Corcoran Gallery of Art, gift of Mr. and Mrs. Lansdell K. Christie, 1959:** Pages 48-49
**Journalism Services:** © Dave Brown: Pages 64-65, 102 (right)
**University of Nebraska Photo Service:** Page 95
**Marilyn Gartman Agency:** © Ellis Herwig: Pages 99, 141
© **R.P. Lindner:** Page 101
**Click/Chicago:** © James R. Simon: Page 108 (bird)
**Nebraska Games & Park Commission:** Page 108 (rocks)
**R/C Photo Agency:** © J.M. Halama: Page 113
**Wide World:** Pages 129 (Brando, Carson, Cather), 130 (Flanagan, Ford), 131 (Malcolm X, Neihardt, Sandoz)
**UPI/Bettmann:** Pages 129 (Bryan), 130 (Fonda)
**Len W. Meents:** Maps on pages 101, 106, 136
**Courtesy Flag Research Center, Winchester, Massachusetts 01890:** Flag on page 108

## About the Author

Jim Hargrove has worked as a writer and editor for more than 10 years. After serving as an editorial director for three Chicago-area publishers, he began a career as an independent writer, preparing a series of books for children. He has contributed to works by nearly 20 different publishers. Some of his Childrens Press titles are *Mark Twain: The Story of Samuel Clemens, Gateway to Freedom: The Story of the Statue of Liberty and Ellis Island, The Story of the Black Hawk War,* and *Microcomputers at Work.* With his wife and teenage daughter, he lives in a small Illinois town near the Wisconsin border.

Hargrove, Jim
Nebraska

## DATE DUE

| | | | |
|---|---|---|---|
| JAN 30 | JAN 18 | MAR 21 | APR 25 |
| JAN 30 | JAN 28 | MAR 28 | |
| JAN 30 | O-5 | APR - 4 | |
| FEB | OCT 23 | APR 11 | |
| FEB | MAR 9 | APR 18 | |
| FEB | MAR 17 | MAY 5 | |
| MAR 30 | FEB 23 | SEP 5 | |
| APR 1 | NOV 2 | OCT 23 | |
| DEC 11 | | DEC 12 | |
| FEB 4 | MAR 7 | DEC 12 | |
| JUN 7 | MAR 14 | JAN 12 | |
| JAN 10 | | | |

OEMCO